The Tarmac and the Trees

by
Dominic Reeve

Illustrations by
Beshlie

D1609986

Lamorna Publications

The Author in his 85th year

Lamorna Publications

Yew Tree Studio, Marshwood, Dorset DT6 5QF
www.lamornapublications.co.uk

First published in 2015

ISBN: 978-0-9933898-0-1

Set in 11pt Times New Roman

Contents

Illustrations

Introduction

In this book (my sixth) I am concentrating to some extent on the numbers and variety of motor-vehicles and trailer-caravans that have passed through our hands since we gave up horses and waggons in their favour some fifty years ago. In many ways I feel more warmly toward those early time-worn motors, even to those that had been ill-served, rather than well-serviced, in the hands of their multifarious previous owners. For such dented rusting wrecks it was no novelty to pay anything from as little as £30 to a maximum of £100.

With the optimism of youth one expected them, like an ill-treated horse, to respond favourably when coming into our possession. In retrospect it was a risky business: sometimes such gambles paid off, whilst others were disastrous. Nonetheless the memory of their differing characters and unexpected performances, even under the most trying of conditions, never fails to gladden my heart.

They were, it goes without saying, *all* "commercials" – we have not ever owned a single saloon car. Our purchases have ranged in size from a miniscule Bradford Jowett van to a 3-ton Bedford T.K. lorry – the latter was needed to pull a heavy and rococo Vickers trailer-caravan which we only kept for a few months.

Alas, so many of them were battered, dented, and rusting colourfully when they came into our possession – utterly worn out, if viewed from the more exacting and precious standards of today. Not for them the indignity of an annual M.O.T. Test – just the occasional chance inspection by a person known as a "nuts and bolts man." The latter, at his own discretion, might on rare sightings legally demand an examination of the motor.

I was but twenty-nine years old when we abandoned our former horse-and-waggon mode of life and took a faltering leap into modernity: it was, in Travellers' terms, a fashionable exercise just then.

Often I feel myself lucky, indeed almost blessed, to have experienced two quite differing ways of living, each overlapping the other.

I venture to hope that by emphasising the importance of the particular type of vehicles embraced by Travellers in their differing occupations I am merely expressing the truth.

In what is known as 'Waggon Times' the breeding, appearance, and performance of one's horses was an ever-present topic of conversation. So it is that today the talk of Travellers is concerning their motors and the development of new models. Not forgetting the new designs of trailers being specifically produced for their delectation.

It seems to me no way illogical for a man to wish to show-off his new motor-vehicle or trailer-caravan with pride, and no more so that it was for his forbears to display their fine horse-drawn turnouts.

In any event I can but hope that this little book, the story of one man's pleasure in achieving gradual improvements in the fashion of his motors and trailers, as symbols of the struggles, my evoke in the reader some small degree of appreciation of the efforts required to remain fixed on the uphill road to..........Arcadia!

DR

Editorial Note

Romani words are printed in italics and are followed by a translation in brackets. Where a *Romani* word has been used frequently, or where the meaning is obvious, the translation may be omitted.

Setting the Scene

Waggon Time – A 'rough and ready' turnout!
(1950s)

Ex US Jeep and first Trailer

Austin Lorry (cost £17.10s)

Ex Fireworks Van – water tank on roof!

(Our first Motor-home)

1956 A Type Bedford Lorry
(Note custom-made Traveller-style 'rack')

Vickers Trailer - side view
(A model from the 1970s)

Chapter 1

Fryern Court

About a mile from the small town of Fordingbridge, on the edge of the New forest, was the house and surrounding grounds of Fryern Court. Within its fastness dwelt the famous and revered artist Augustus John. Although he had almost achieved the dubious honour of becoming an octogenarian by the time we first met, none of his faculties (apart from some loss of hearing) appeared to have become impaired. Tall and erect with piercing blue eyes, bearded like an hidalgo, with flowing white locks beneath a broad-brimmed straw hat, he was still an imposing figure to behold. At Fryern he was invariably clad in loose-fitting blue denim trousers and the sort of jacket once favoured by the firemen on steam locomotives; it was for comfort rather than smartness that he strove. His shirts (which would undeniably have been frowned upon by the directors of Turnbull & Asser) were colour-splashed tartan checks of adventurous hues. As an added bonus he often donned a silk scarf, knotted *diklo*-style at his throat, possibly in symbolic reference to his lifelong interest in the Romani people, whose language he could speak with surprising fluency. About him still lingered hints of the dandyism of his past.

In his later years he rarely strayed from the confines of Fryern, apart from very occasional business trips to London, his presence and charisma seemed to reverberate through both Fordingbridge and the surrounding villages. Indeed older residents would often recall with heart-felt nostalgia and pleasure – not to say astonishment – some of his more bucolic escapades in a society lost forever.

Fryern Court was an elegant and spacious old house, ochre-coloured and pleasing to the eye. Although in a faintly dilapidated condition at first glance, closer inspection would show it to be merely a little time-worn and in no danger of falling down!

It was reached by a longish gravel driveway, bending in around some bushes before the house, which was scarcely visible from the road. On the left hand side, some fifty yards before the house itself, there stood the 'New Studio.' It was brick-built, standing on concrete pillars, thus being twelve or fifteen feet above the ground. Entrance was afforded by ascending a flight of stairs. With a flat roof, walls both curved and straight, and vast windows, I personally did not find it especially attractive, though I am sure that it served its purpose well.

Numerous fine works were produced within its hallowed walls, and many were the fascinating models who fell under the romantic and mesmeric spell exerted upon them by one of our finest artists.

It had replaced the 'Old Studio' some years before. The latter was to be found by the diligent searcher in overgrown seclusion some distance from the rear of the house and could only be approached by means of a narrow footpath. This path, and the studio, had, over the course of time, fought a losing battle with rapacious creepers, bushes, and trees, becoming all but swamped by foliage. At the time of which I am writing (late 1950s) Augustus was using it solely for working on a gigantic, lyrically-inspired, Triptych, toiling on it sporadically as and when the fit took him. It was a task which seemed to be never-ending, causing him little but dissatisfaction, especially as its progression became slower and slower. Apparently no sooner had he completed one or two of the ethereal, nay angelic, figures pursuing their esoteric and mystical rites than uncertainty about their form would grip him. He would then over-paint them into obliteration, only to commence his labours anew. During the rest of his life this unhappy state of mind prevailed. The completion was denied to us.

During a short stay at Fryern a year previously, the artist had commenced working on a large full-length portrait of Beshlie, wearing a long blue floral dress; he was hoping to complete it without delay and start on another, this time to be in a red dress and, of course, in a characteristically dramatic pose. Beshlie herself, detached and faintly aloof, was an ideal sitter – she almost seemed to have a 'John face.' It was a time of wonder and excitement for us.

So it was that in the late summer of 1959 we were stopping in a field adjoining the house. It was well over an acre with plenty of grazing for the horses, and was bordered on three sides by thick and lofty hedges, thus affording us privacy from any passing traffic, for the sight of us may have aroused suspicion in those for whom a horse and waggon was an unacceptable intrusion. There were just our horse and waggon and a little tub-cart and small pony.

Alas, however, despite our delight in the portraits of Beshlie, our lives were, at that point, filled with some trepidation. Of our own doing, this state of mind was occasioned by the fact of us deciding to become mechanised – in the form of motor vehicle and trailer caravan. It was a decision that was being taken by myriad Travellers just then – many deserting brightly painted waggons and fine coloured horses for ugly little box-like trailers and motors of dubious parentage. Many of the latter being 'cut-down' saloon cars with little lorry bodies added in order that they could be used for earning a living. It was a strange and rather unhappy period when everyone was trying to adapt themselves to a 'motor and trailer' style of life. Several years were to pass before Travellers succeeded in stamping their own personalities on to their possessions. For many years the Bedford lorry: firstly the 'Bull-nose,' then the A-type, bulbous and squat; then came the J-type, American-influenced and a pleasure to drive. Later, for those who required a larger vehicle for their work, or for the towing of the huge, elaborately decorated, 'Vickers' and 'Westmorland Star' trailers, the bigger Bedford TK was favoured. Soon to be manufactured only with diesel engines as petrol prices increased, these forward-control monsters were highly esteemed.

Our final decision was, at least to some extent, governed by my ability to pass the Driving Test. As someone who had faithfully avoided all forms of tests throughout my life from the age of ten, its novelty value appealed to the more bizarre side of my character.

I knew nothing whatsoever about engines, on even the simplest level: spark plugs, ignition, cylinders, even main bearings and fly-wheels conjured up little excitement. I recollect when a Traveller friend recently became the proud owner of an ancient 1937 Bedford 30 cwt lorry: I was faintly disturbed when he announced that it was ailing.

"Ar," he pronounced with authority, "Ball-race trouble, I shouldn't wonder." A condition surely guaranteed to unnerve all but the sturdiest of drivers.

In any event our minds were made up. Hence, with some degree of wisdom, I enrolled myself on a driving-lessons course at a branch in Salisbury of a well-known firm with offices all over the country.

To take the Driving Test in a car with their logo emblazoned upon it might, I hoped, cause a favourable impression in the mind of the examiner. At least, I trusted, he would presume that I had been correctly advised on the rudiments of road safety.

Upon arriving for my first lesson I was a little unbalanced by the aspect of my instructor. He was, in fact, a classic example of a youngish ex-army officer, the war behind him, entering a field of employment which seemed strangely at odds with his social standing: it was a sad mirror of the times. He was a rather elegant man, wearing pale cavalry-twill trousers, suede 'chukka' boots, and an expensively tailored check jacket which would surely have been applauded in the smartest of equestrian circles. His fair hair, carefully groomed, was beginning to recede, whilst his rather florid features were tastefully livened by the presence of a curiously dark well-trimmed moustache.

Nevertheless, after the first two lessons his manner grew to something quite near to amiability, almost docility. Thus, after several action-packed excursions in one of the school's Morris 1000 saloons my confidence and enthusiasm grew. I began to find that I *liked* driving! At that time I had no way of realising that the Morris 1000 was one of the easiest cars to manage, capable of a surprising turn of speed, even in a forward direction! After what seemed to me to be a pleasingly short space of time the chain-smoking instructor suggested that I might be capable of attempting to take the Test in Salisbury. The fine weather of that autumn was still holding on the day of my trial. I recollected riding there by bicycle, on an aged sit-up-and-beg Sunbeam which I was lent by an agreeable old gentlewoman who resided near to Fryern. After a journey of about half an hour to the Cathedral City I met my instructor as arranged, and we arrived at the Test Centre at the appointed time.

The Test Examiner, in dark suit and 'car-coat,' was a man of no immediate charisma but, perhaps surprisingly, his nature did not seem to have become soured by his unrewarding, even tedious, occupation.

He smiled encouragingly at me and we took our respective places within the little saloon; a pad with official-looking documents resting comfortably on his knee.

Despite having been urged by 'the Major' to memorise all the information contained in the Highway Code (including braking distances and every road sign shown within) the slightly blasé examiner asked me only *one* question (concerning hand signals) which came as a slight disappointment to me, having been cross-questioned by Beshlie the previous evening and learning 90% of the Code by heart!

And so it was that after nothing more stressful than a three-point turn, a hill-start, and an 'emergency stop,' we were back at the Test Centre and I was informed that I had passed!

My instructor, who was seated on a low wall enjoying the sun, smoking as always, greeted my good news with a guarded smile which gave away little of his feelings. His spirits appeared to lift, however, when I assured him that I would direct a letter to his Head Office, fulsome in its praise of his tuition and apprising his superiors that my success was due solely to his teaching skills. We parted in friendly fashion, and the next day I did compose a praise-filled missive and despatched as promised.

Once back at Fryern Court, leg-muscles aching from the cycling exertions, and head whirling from the stress, I was able to impart the welcome news of my triumph to Beshlie. I had been presented with a paper on which it was stated that my Full Licence would be despatched to me shortly, and that the form would be sufficient to authorise me to drive until it arrived. In fact, it reached me within a week and, upon inspection, revealed that it would not expire until the year 2000 – my seventieth birthday. An incomprehensible journey into the future it seemed then. Looking back, alas, is an easier mission. Upon my returning home with the unexpected result we both agreed that we should, with the minimum of delay, set about the complications of exchanging four legs for four wheels, hence propelling ourselves into what was then the twentieth century and all that it entailed. The pony and tub-cart would be easy to sell. Neither ranked especially high in our affections; the pony, although quiet in traffic, was of uncertain temper, strong-willed and hard-mouthed. Ill treatment from a previous owner had destroyed his trust in humanity.

We had purchased him, and the harness and tub-cart, from an aged Romani horse-dealer. He was well-known to me, as were many of his relatives with whom we had travelled in the West Country. He had himself been settled-down for some years in Dorset. He resided, on a small piece of land that he had bought, in an agreeable looking tow-roomed cabin with a tall stove-pipe protruding from the roof. At that time his spirits were a little low having but recently lost his ancient wife of over fifty years. She was named Miella, whom I rarely encountered except at horse-fairs, to which she seemed as addicted as her husband, both generally becoming fully intoxicated by the end of the day. Once a fine-looking and handsome Romani woman she became, in later years, cross-hatched of feature, black complexioned, gnarled, and lame. The last condition, which she described as a 'mortified leg' necessitated the use of a stout blackthorn stick to assist her walking. If annoyed by the sight of any passer-by whose look she decided was condescending, or if merely in the grip of a malicious mood, she was likely to threaten them with the cudgel. Her expertise in performing such a frightening ritual was effective on even the most sullen of persons, and none but the most retarded could fail to show respect in the face of such an onslaught.

"God's cuss you!" she would shout, her filmy eyes still managing to glitter with fury, and her time-worn voice harsh like a wounded raven, "I'll lay me stick about y'ears!" Alas, yet one more sight and sound to be missed.

However, her husband still continued his business ventures after her death, despite constantly bewailing her passing. Elevating her, in her final absence, to an almost Goddess-like stature.

This came as a faint surprise to those for whom the couple's long-term marital conflicts, and even ferocious physical battles, had become the stuff of legend. Even their six offspring, and numerous grandchildren had spent their lives taking sides, provoking even more continuous strife.

As we were uninvolved emotionally with both the pony and the tub-cart we were willing to sell to the highest bidder. However, our feelings differed considerably regarding our waggon-horse, and indeed the waggon too. Our waggon-horse was the best that we had ever owned: a shapely, stocky, Welsh Cob mare. She stood about 15 hands in height, with a thick, curving, 'rainbow' neck, and was barely eight years old. A glossy dark bay, with four white feet, she would pull any waggon with willingness and placidity: not 'nappy' or a 'bouncer!' On top of that she remained utterly unfazed by motor traffic of any sort, even steamrollers. Many a Traveller could have spent half of his life in seeking out such an animal. It is said that every horse has its 'dodge,' often to be discovered by the owner's cost. In the case of Whitefeet it remained an un-divulged secret to us – even after five years of ownership. We were undoubtedly grieved at the thought of parting from her; we could only decide to be especially particular about the person to whom we would sell her.

The waggon, the last we were to inhabit, was a 'Dorset' Open-lot. Square-bowed, as opposed to the more romantic 'Barrel-top' shape, it was a well-constructed if not ornate waggon. At least it had wooden, iron-bonded wheels, and not pneumatic car wheels – a regrettable trend at that time. It was not by any means, however, amongst the better, craftsmen-built by famous and

'Dorset' Open-lot

revered builders, that had passed through our hands in the past decades.

I decided that, as we were not pressed for time and were welcome to stay on at Fryern in the hopes that the portrait could be finished, I would place an advertisement in the For Sale columns of a well-known rural newspaper, the circulation of which spread over most of the West Country, offering a remarkable diversity of articles and advertisements – thus answering the needs of both the humblest and the most opulent in society, with especial leanings toward those of a rustic inclination – discerning to a man.

In passing I might mention that its reporting of minor court cases could frequently brighten what might have been a gloomy day. I remember perusing one edition's inclusion of two especially bizarre reports which must, surely, have caused many a resident in sheltered subtopia to ingest their breakfast porridge with some difficulty.

One account described the behaviour of two farmhands, in their late twenties, who were each accused of "performing indecent acts of unnatural perversion" upon a hitherto docile goat belonging to a neighbouring cottager, for which offences they were both sentenced to jail terms (although, apparently, no complaint was received from the goat!).

The same magistrate, by that time surely somewhat dispirited, was later faced by an itinerant Irish labourer of fairly advanced years. He was charged with the somewhat unusual offence of "being indecently clad in torn clothing whilst walking along the main street of Dorchester, causing distress to innocent passers-by, which could have led to a breach of the peace." Bucolic of complexion and perspiring profusely, we were told, he appeared highly indignant at the accusation against him, and in no way penitent.

"Ah Jesus, Your Worship, Sir, de whole t'ing is rubbish! If I wants to go about with me arse hangin' out've me trousers then I'll do – I swear to God it's me own business. Ah, Blessed Lord above I t'ought dis was a free country, so I did."

At such a defiant lack of remorse the magistrates displayed little sympathy – not even the offer of a newer less rended pair of trousers. With the wisdom of their mean judgement they fined him £20 – to be paid within fourteen days.

By the faithful recording of such trivia, safe in the knowledge that it would be favoured by the majority of its readers, did this excellent organ of culture and information annually increase its sales.

A day or so later, our food supplies dwindling, I embarked on a journey to the commissariat in Fordingbridge. Reaching the High Street I perceived a small group of local Forest Romanies in conversation. They were, with one exception, settled-down in one or other of the little encampments locally dotted about. These mainly comprised ramshackle shacks of corrugated iron, some with old canvas sheeting for added protection; the sort of accommodation now to be found only in slum townships in the 'Third World' – yet then regarded as being quite good enough for the once roaming Travellers, born and bred in the New Forest, their freedom stolen from them by the dead hand of Authority. A familiar figure detached himself from the others at my approach. It was a young man known as 'Jacky Owls' who was one of the last full-time 'bender' tent dwellers left in that part of the country. He was swarthy and shabby, an old black hat atop even blacker curls, a coloured neckerchief knotted at his throat. An ancient check jacket, russet corduroy trousers and down-at-heel jodhpur boots of un-polished tan colour, all amalgamated to convey a picture of 'The Gypsy.' His appearance found no disfavour in my eyes.

"Hello my old kid," he greeting me affably, and we shook hands.

"Where are you stopping, Jacky?" I enquired. It was a polite question, expected.

"We'm out at Dinilo's Corner agen Fir Wood," he replied.

He was, he went on to say, staying with his in-laws, bender – dwellers all their married lives. It was, I felt, owing to his wife's unwillingness to adapt to waggon in favour of their more old-fashioned accommodation which had enticed him. With but a pony and small cart or trap they were able to transport themselves and their few possessions with ease and lack of complications. I was inevitably reminded of the old Traveller's ballad:

"When we stops travelling, the first thing in mind
Tis tent-rods and ridge-poles we now got to find.
We tied the old pony's legs, but away he did go.
Where shall we find him? The Lord only knows.
We got up next morning and searched all around.
Where did we find him? We found him in pound.
We *jalled* (went) to the old *rai (gent)*, and what did he say?
Pack up your old trap – and clear right away!"

However, it transpired to be a meeting of mutual advantage. Life was on a seemingly downward spiral just then for Jacky.

"I'm fucked right up, old kid," he confided. "I've just had to have me little pony shot, cos he've had his two dear back-legs, broke like carrots, by an old farmer's gurt *gry* (horse). I put me pony in the *poove* (field) t'other *rati* (night). I never knowed about the old farmer's *gri* bein' in there. When I comes to get him out in the morning he was led there half *mullo* (dead). The best pony I've ever had – I wouldn't took £300 for him. Anyways I had to get old 'Skin-and-Bones' (the nickname of a local abattoir owner) to come and shoot him and take him on for the fucking glue factory. Not wuth a light what he paid me – no wonder they calls him 'Skin an' Bones.'"

After listening with sympathy to the tale of disaster, my mind strayed to the old adage, 'One man's misfortune is another's good fortune.' It seemed likely that, quite unexpectedly, I may have found a buyer for our pony, if not the harness and tub-cart too. And so it was that I felt it incumbent upon me to offer him the opportunity to replace his pony, and harness, and tub-cart as well if he so wished. His reaction was, as would have been expected, cautious and non-committal. But I was encouraged by his suggestion of walking back with me to Fryern to inspect the goods.

"Well my old Jacky," I observed, "your eyes are your guide. If you don't like what you see then don't buy – no harm done."

During the course of the two-mile trudge back home I apprised him of our plans for immediate mechanisation as I had passed the Driving Test. His response was to react with considerable pessimism – though whether genuine or affected I could not quite puzzle out. At that time Travellers were abandoning horse-drawn waggons with enthusiasm, so he may have felt a little left-behind.

"It takes a good man to keep a moty on the road," he stated with conviction. "I seen many a fellow ruin hisself with the expenses of moties," he declared mournfully, adding for good measure: "Me cousin Caleb, old Sonner's boy, had the best waggon and horses as money could buy. A lovely turnout. However, he was down-country travelling, and doing well – plenty to eat and a nice bit of *loover* (money) as well. Then one day he gets in a *kitchema* (Public House) wi' some of they London Travellers, fly old boys, an' he done no more'n *chop* (swap) the lot away for an old lorry and trailer – an' gid a few pound notes as well. And him with no licence nor nothin'. Anyway he don't take no notice of that. Murders when he get home an' sez what he've done. Well, like me dead mother, next day he no sooner drives ten mile up the road in the old lorry when the fuckin' ingine blowed-up! Finished! They was stopped on an old layby with no means to *jal* (go). Then down comes the rain an' they find the trailer roof leaking like a sieve! *Pani* (water) everywhere. By all accounts you never seen nothin' like it. His three little *chavies* (children) cryin' their *yoks* (eyes) out an' his dear wife *delling* (hitting) him with a lump of wood! On my life it took him near on a twelvemonth to get back on his feet with a *kushti* (good) waggon an' a *bori* (big) strong cob to pull 'em about. He ain't too bad now, but I can take oath as he won't never give up the old ways agen, never no more."

"Oh dear, what can you say? Bad luck for the man," was all I could reply. It was not really the kind of story that I had hoped for at the juncture in my life.

Just before reaching Fryern I managed to bring my mind into focussing on the immediate matter in hand. I thus began to extol the virtues, both true and imagined, of the little turnout which I was about to present for his approval. In truth the pony was a snappy little mover, traffic-proof and of some stamina. He was a dappled grey, around 12 hands high and only six years old: only his temper could be faulted. But luckily that was not a condition that would trouble the average Traveller in those days. The set of harness was not ornate but was sound, and the same could be said for the little tub, or governess, cart – smart, in black and coach-lined in red.

"A pretty pony," I remarked encouragingly.

"He don't look too bad," assented Jacky, inhaling and coughing bronchially on a roll-up Black Beauty cigarette of enticing thinness, its acrid though strangely sweet odour surrounding us. Smoking was a habit that I had but lately renounced.

Gathering a halter from beside the harness hanging of the side of the cart we strode purposefully and directly up to the pony, the halter soon about his head. To catch a horse in a field the direct approach must be adopted; hesitation or gesticulation will invariably cause the animal, no matter how tractable, to evade capture by even the most amiable of owners. After a cursory examination of the pony's feet, and a more careful inspection of his teeth, Jacky suggested that we put him 'in' – that is to say harness him up and drive him around the field in the cart.

The latter was accomplished with no aggravation – he was always without any apparent objection in the matter. I write as one who has experienced horrors in the past, of animals unwilling to be harnessed or backed into the shafts, or, worse still, 'Bouncers' (kickers). The latter wrought havoc on many a cart, and even waggons, by breaking shafts with their well-aimed hooves – on occasions destroying the fronts of the vehicles for good measure. An alarming activity to behold.

Leaping into the tub-cart with an agile bound Jacky set off at a good pace, applying a few light blows with a hazel switch as an encouragement to the pony to increase his speed from a moderate trot. This he did with an immediacy of action which might have discommoded a less experienced driver. Jacky, however, merely laughed, lauding the pony and urging it to even greater speed until it was moving at something approaching full gallop. I watched with some interest: philosophical as to what the outcome might be. To extract sufficient money from Jacky to make a deal would, I sensed, be akin to a convulsion if not handled with restraint.

After two laps around the field he jumped wordlessly from the tub-cart. Silently we un-harnessed the pony and let him loose, at which, after a few paces, he rolled to and fro on his back – casting somewhat malevolent stares in our direction. His temper, as always, uncertain.

Beshlie was seated on the footboard of the waggon enjoying the early autumn sunlight, the fire a few yards on the ground in front of her, the kettle-iron hovering over the embers.

"Let's go over and have a cup of tea and a talk," I suggested.

Jacky readily agreed, and within a few minutes I had built up the stick fire, the kettle soon singing amidst the flames. Beshlie made the tea in an old decorated enamel teapot which had been given to us by some old-fashioned Travellers when she had expressed an admiration for it.

Decorated enamel teapot

The drink soon brewed, and served in floral patterned mugs, with plenty of sugar and a little tinned milk, it comprised a pleasing and distinctive beverage. (In future years, enjoying the refinements of more gracious living, and oftentimes abandoning the outside *yog* (fire) for the alternative indoor bottled-gas cooker, something was lost in the taste of both food and drink.)

It was twelve noon and I envisaged a few hours to be spent haggling, if indeed the possibility of a deal arose. Seated by the fireside, the combined scents of wood smoke and Black Beauty, in the presence of this essentially Romani man beside me I was momentarily cast into doubt about our impending transference to the worship and solace of the internal combustion engine. Logic, however, pointed towards the wisdom of our decision: all the accoutrements of the old life-style, even reliable working horses, were disappearing – their replacements being harder and harder to discover. This was, of course, the late 'fifties and the renaissance of the craft of waggon-building, and the re-breeding of heavy cobs to draw them, had not yet materialised. Ironically enough, it is easier to obtain a turnout of high quality today in the 2000s than was the case in the late'50s, strange and hardly believable though it may seem!

"How much is you gonna axe me for that dee-little pony, kid?" Jacky suddenly enquired directly.

To allow myself room to manoeuvre it was necessary for me to voice a figure higher than I would actually accept.

"Well, he's a good quiet pony – you wouldn't find a better," I replied, before answering his question: "I'll take £50 for him, but if you want to give me £90 I'll throw in the tub-cart and the set of harness."

"How much?" he said, affecting a grimace of pain at the proposition. "I'll tell you what, no harm, kid, but £40 should oughta buy the lot! Like me dead father I wouldn't gie you no £90."

I poured out another mug of tea and Jacky skilfully rolled yet another matchstick-thin cigarette, lit it with a brand from the fire, and inhaled deeply, coughing bronchially the while. It was, I could see, going to be a long drawn-out negotiation, though one which I felt might eventually reach a conclusion of moderate satisfaction to us both. I was at a slight advantage in so far as I was in no way forced into a sale at that stage, whereas Jacky was in dire need after the misfortune of losing his own pony.

And so it was, like a slowed down game of tennis, our offers being batted to and fro over the course of an hour, that tensions rose – a climax, or anti-climax, was close.

I eventually coaxed him into the belief (by no means untrue) that his best deal would be achieved by his purchasing the whole turnout. His final offer ("on my baby's life I wouldn't gie you no more") was £60. In valuation terms this comprised £45 for the pony and £15 for the tub-cart and harness. (Ludicrous by today's prices but quite reasonable then.) Our palms met to clinch the deal and, to my no great surprise, Jacky reached into his pocket and produced a wad of somewhat crushed-looking notes. He peeled off the requisite number of pound-notes and ten-pound notes – carefully counting them out on the ground. I handed him one pound back for the traditional 'luck money' and he was ready to go, our waggon-horse watching the proceedings with curiosity.

From then on, in a surprisingly rapid turn of events we became the owner of our first motor vehicle. After one or two fruitless missions I happened upon the yard of an elderly Traveller, many of whose relations were known to me, and most of whom were, like us, in the maelstrom of adapting to motorisation in the form of lorries or vans. His yard was surrounded by ten feet high corrugated-iron sheeting, topped with barbed-wire, and was filled with an interesting selection of 'commercials' ranging from cut-down cars, and small vans – most still bearing the names and occupations of their previous owners inscribed upon them. The mid-size, and larger, motors were parked nose-outwards to one side: they were all, almost without exception, of makes and weight-carrying capacities which would appeal to Travellers. There were several little 15cwt Fordson lorries, one especially entrancing in pea-green and lined-out and 'scrolled' in bright red. It had, its signs boasted, belonged to a General Dealer. I was taken with its appearance but was forced to admit to myself that, with a 3-speed gearbox as an added disincentive, it would scarcely be powerful enough to drag all but the most miniscule of trailers in its wake. Moving further along, noticing the black-suited figure of Old Alf, the patriarch who, with his obese son Young Alf, operated the business together from an office hut, whilst living in a splendidly appointed caravan which was partly shielded from public gaze by a breeze-block wall.

My eye was caught by a rather well-preserved 30cwt Bull-nose Bedford van of 1946 vintage. A refined grey, with red wheels, in colouration, it did not show much sign of having endured a very rough passage during its years of toil. The evidence of 'fillers,' ill-repaired panelling, and the like were hard to discern and indeed the killer-rust, the scourge of vans, had not exerted a visible hold. Only its mileage seemed to be against it. After going 'round the clock' once it would seem that the experience enthused the last owner to embark on a second such journey: the mileometer indicated 194,000 miles.

Perceiving my interest Old Alf proceeded slowly towards me. Wearing an old black trilby, black tweed suit and coloured silk scarf, he appeared disinterested in contemporary fashion. His features were pointed and heavily lined, his complexion pitted and scarred, whilst his eyes, both running in sympathy for each other, were glittering and black under his hat brim.

"How be you, my boy," he greeted me, adding, "I seen you before somewhere, down one o' they horse-sales I shouldn't wonder."

"The last one I was at was at Wimborne – the Wimborne Block. I was with Old Johnny and Eli, your brother, I think," I mused.

"You'm right, young man. Eli is me youngest brother – one o' the finest step-dancers down that country. Is you after a motor, young man? 'cos if you is we can fix you up. My Alfie'll be back directly. You can surely have a deal wi' him." Indeed as he finished speaking a smart Bedford lorry drew up in the yard. It was an A-type model, its exterior newly-painted in a fetching combination of vivid red and contrasting maroon, no more than four years old, with a strong tell-tale 'step' tow-bar much favoured by Travellers of those times.

Young Alf, in his late thirties, was balding and overweight; he had dark Romani eyes and puffy features. He was clad in a curious mixture of sartorial motifs: a heavy collarless shirt of the sort once favoured by farm workers, a corduroy waistcoat too small to cover his burgeoning paunch, pin-stripe trousers, and tan-coloured jodhpur boots.

Yet despite this array of disadvantages there hung about him an air of natural benevolence which could not have failed to help him in his business dealings. With his considerable rotundity he fitted in well with the rounded, almost bulbous design of the Bedford A-type. Emerging from the cab he greeted me with a hand-shake and the customary: "Where's you out at?"

Apprising him of our location I enquired of the van.

"No flies on you, mate," he smiled. "Best old van on the place – come off a fireworks firm, no Travellers ain't owned un."

In those days such a recommendation was to be welcomed. As, many being utterly inexperienced in the rudimentary requirements of engines, would offer them no form of servicing or attention.

The wonderfully sentimental adage in common usage was: "Keep un topped-up with oil and water – she'll soon tell ee when she'm out of petrol."

To many a beginner-motorist of that era it seemed all the erudition required. "Start her up, let's hear how she runs," I suggested – though with little hope that I would give the correct interpretation to any existent faults. In any event, Alf heaved himself into the cab, turned on the ignition and pulled on the self-starter, simultaneously drawing out the choke to its fullest extent.

To, I think, the private astonishment of us both, we heard the engine fire and, with what I later came to realise was the special tone of those old six-cylinder Bedford petrol engines, it ticked-over smoothly.

"Sweet as a nut," observed Young Alf, beaming at me.

"Can I have a drive?" I requested, to which he readily assented. His only question being: "You got a *slang* (licence) ain't you?"

On receiving my affirmative reply he promptly drew the van from between its compatriots, facing it toward the exit from the yard.

"Go up the road here, then turn left down by the *kitchema* and left agen by the big old yew-tree an' you'll be back here."

Entering the cab I was struck by the odour, later to become familiar to me in all elderly lorries it seemed, of petrol, leather-cloth and oil; mellow and comforting to the judicious driver.

In those days, and with certain kinds of customer-friendly dealers, excellent men unwilling to allow themselves to be bound by legalities, there were areas of give-and-take in their actions toward more favoured purchasers – the like of which is rarely practised by their more factory-produced colleagues today with their shiny shoes and clip-boards.

Having never, at that point, encountered the 'crash' gearbox I realised that it was not a thing to be advertised. Hence I left the yard at a snail's pace, in first gear, changing up to second at a still slow speed. From then on I was out of sight or sound of Alf, who thankfully was unable to hear the grinding of cogs, splutters and bangs of objection, from the protesting gearbox, until I finally managed to engage the third gear and, as the ultimate achievement, managed the fourth, cruising along the country back-road at a steady 30mph. Turning onto the stretch of main road, however, overtaken by the spirit of adventure, I increased the speed to a nerve straining 60mph. It was the fastest I had ever travelled. Even the little Morris 1000 had not been known to exceed 50mph and then only with a favourable tail-wind! Like Toad of Toad Hall I could feel the shadow of speed-addiction hovering over me. I would have to fight it. Slowing down I followed the route Young Alf had decreed, turning by the public house, and was soon back at the yard. As I arrived I perceived that both men were standing by the little office-shed, both smoking roll-up cigarettes, though of greater dimensions than those produced by Jacky.

"We thought you'd a-gone an' *chored* (stolen) un," laughed Young Alf.

"Never in this world," said his father, feigning disapproval at such a suggestion.

"I knows a good man from a fuckin' *chorer* (thief) – I kin read a man be just lookin' at him. What's more, young man, I knows we'll have a deal – even if you robs us blind," he concluded, his eyes twinkling.

"How much are you going to ask me?" I enquired, knowing that there's no love in dealing and that I would have to struggle.

"Let's go up in the trailer, an' my poor old wife'll make us a nice dish to tea, an' we can see what can be done," continued Old Alf.

The trailer was a 20ft Eccles Traveller, cream in colour and shining, with blue-painted ends: it was the Traveller's 'in-fashion' trailer of the moment – before the Vickers and the Westmorland Stars with their splendidly rococo exteriors.

Although, if spotted in the streets, Old Alf might well have been presumed by the uninitiated to have been but a poor old gypsy man, closer examination would have pointed toward his actual prosperity. His brown, scallop-patterned boots were of the highest quality, as was his tweed suit; whilst on a least two of his fingers there gleamed gold rings with inset diamonds. And should he smile several gold teeth would be displayed – all adornments which met with my strong approval.

As we entered the trailer we were met by the matriarch Leander, who although crippled by rheumatism, showed vestiges of the beauty which must once have drawn Alf to her. Her hair, still black, was worn in two braids, her strong hawk-like nose, and her eyes, like those of Young Alf, were a glittering and unfathomable black. Sadly, to my way of thinking, she had abandoned the old fashions of Romani dress for a smart blouse and skirt which, were reminiscent of upper middle-class ladies intent on their own uniforms. Thankfully, at least, these unadventurous fashions were enlivened by the presence of heavy gold jewellery looped and pinned about her person.

"Give this young man a cup of tea, 'oman," Old Alf instructed her, and we sat down on the striped leather bunks, our backs supported by hand-embroidered velvet cushions. The trailer was graced by a 'Parkway' coal-burning stove which was, in the manner of Travellers, heaped to capacity with glowing red coals.

"I likes a warm trailer – I can't abear to be cold," pronounced Old Alf, impervious to the heat.

All around the trailer were glass fronted display cupboards and lockers too – each filled with Royal Worcester or Crown Derby China in a profusion greater than I had ever beheld. It was a pleasure to witness such opulence. We drank our tea slowly from Crown Derby mugs. Young Alf sat alone at the far end of the trailer and was the first to broach the subject of my visit.

"What do you think about the van, *mush* (man)? Would he do for you?"

"Depends what you're asking," I replied cautiously.

"I'd take £150 for 'un," said Alf, gazing steadily at me.

"Oh dear," I replied, "I couldn't do that – I'll give you £80 cash, now!"

"Oh my dear Blessed Lord!" exclaimed Alf, affecting shock. "Did you hear that, Father?"

"I thanks you for makin' a bid, young man – one bidder's worth a hundred lookers-on, as me old father used to say," replied Old Alf, rolling a Black Beauty cigarette, and one for his stiff-fingered old wife.

"You could go all over the country an' you wouldn't find a better van for its age. I wouldn't tell you a lie, *mush*; I'd walk to the end of the world an' back 'fore I'd tell you a lie. The old motor's so good as new – with every bit of service done on un since new – just the one owner. I tell you what I'll do, if you's a serious buyer, I'll …..I'll tek

22

£125, only cos me Dad likes you, an' I wouldn't be makin' hardly a penny."

"Hark here," I smiled. "Anyone'd have to get up early to put anything over on you!"

Young Alf smiled, flattered I could see.

"I'll tell you what I'll do," I began, encouragingly. "I'll give you £100 and you give me back a fiver for luck – the money's in my pocket."

"We ain't a-worried about that, young man," observed Old Alf, continuing: "We ain't a-worried about you payin' for un – you kin gie us the money anytime once we've had a deal."

Yet more flattery, this time from Old Alf, secure in the knowledge that I would not call his bluff.

"Thank you for your offer, but I couldn't do it," said Young Alf, his face a picture of innocent regret.

"If I was to take offers like that I'd soon be out of business," he complained. "And me dear old Mam and Dad'd be starving!"

"Yes, I can see that," I replied, poising myself for another, possibly final, offer.

"Well, I'll try and have a deal with you," I began. Both father and son gazed in anticipation, whilst Leander, disinterested, commenced to wash the mugs in soapy water in a stainless-steel bowl. Old Leander paused in her washing-up, the two men continuing to stare expectantly at me.

I liked the van. I wanted the van – a deal must be done. I adopted my most serious expression and spoke:

"Now, here's my very best offer, and I won't go any higher – I'll take an oath on that! I'll give you £110 here and now and drive the old van away. Yes or no?"

Young Alf's features temporarily lost their benevolent expression. " Well it looks like we ain't goin' to have a deal ….."

"I never seed two fellers like it," grumbled Old Alf in assumed exasperation. "We shall be yere till midnight 'fore you twos has a deal – too slow for me."

Young Alf rose and started toward the trailer door. At the last moment pausing and wheeling round dramaticallty.

"Here's me last word, on me mam's life I wouldn't take no less," he announced with some fervour. "Gimme £115 an' the motor's yours – the bestest deal you've ever had."

I was happy at that result and our palms met in settlement. Immediately the atmosphere was relaxed and we enjoyed a further cup of tea as I counted out the notes, £100 in tens and three in fives – one of the last being handed back to me 'for luck' in the old-fashioned dealer's custom.

"She'm taxed till the end of the month an' you can fix yourself up wi' a bit of 'surance an' that, I'm certain," said Alf, in the more free and easy circumstances prevailing in those happier motoring times. It was a nice little deal, a pleasure in itself, and as I drove away from the yard I felt it to have been a day well-spent.

I enjoyed a placid and uneventful journey back to Fryern, miraculously performing the neurosis-causing actions of double de-clutching on no fewer than three occasions. For one of so little experience it was indeed a feat in itself: a memory to treasure!

As I drove into the field at Fryern Beshlie was on her way back from the New Studio, where she had been sitting for several hours as Augustus continued his work on the portrait: 'The Girl in the Floral Dress.' The latter was long, full-skirted, and romantic-looking, utterly suited to the requirements of a John picture.

Beshlie went up into the waggon to change out of the dress. She emerged wearing an exotic skirt that she had made by the sewing-together of a quantity of men's cotton 'snuff handkerchiefs' in a multiplicity of colouration and design, a hand-sewn blouse and decorated waistcoat. With long blonde hair and splashy earrings combined with such clothing it would have been difficult for even the most ardent student of sociology to pinpoint her position on the ladder.

The Bedford van met with her approval and we pondered on what it might hold in store for us, and what our immediate plans should be before winter set in.

Taking stock of our possessions we found that we owned the waggon and horse, an Alsatian dog, and a Bantam cock-bird and two hens and a canary. In some ways thankful we were low on livestock. Our priority was, we decided, to sell Whitefeet and her harness, keeping hold of the waggon for the time being. As has so often happened in my life Fate was to take a hand.

The very next morning we were interrupted by the blowing of a motor-horn at the field gate. Investigation showed me a small ex-Royal Mail van, hand-painted in a tasteful brown shade. In the driver's seat was a 'dealing man' (an interesting breed of men who, without visible means of subsistence and in no regular employment, eked out a living solely by buying and selling of 'all sorts,' or by taking commission on any transaction in which they had engineered the meeting of the two participants). Named Gilly Gayle, he was of a rather frenetic disposition, and in features resembled something of a cross between Clarke Gable and George Formby. Alas, however, not possessing the burly stature of the former or the ukulele-playing talents of the latter, he was not necessarily advantaged. He lived in a hut some miles from Fordingbridge, on a small patch of apparent wasteland of which, just then, he was claiming ownership by means of 'Squatters' Rights!' As he had been residing there for a dozen or more years it was deemed likely that he would be successful in his attempt. One hoped so.

In some ways, however, he was his own enemy by reason of his strange fascination for hoarding. The objects that he gathered into his possession were multifarious in size and nature, ranging from old motor bodies, furniture and building detritus, down to mounds of bottles and jars, and paraphernalia of every imaginable variety. When his craving for 'stock' was at its worst he was known to remove van-loads of actual rubbish from the nearest Council Tip – the workers thereon, often scavengers themselves, were apparently so over-awed by this strange little figure's ability to raise the talent of the true scavenger almost to an art-form that they found themselves too impressed to object.

As I neared the gate he emerged from the van which was characteristically laden-down by its contents, appearing, to my casual glance, to have been the result of one of his habitual rubbish-dump visits. Neither a snappy-dresser nor a believer in ablutions, other than on a half-yearly basis, he was especially unsavoury if encountered in a facing-wind. Luckily on that particular day this was not the case. I could not help but speculate on the reaction that might have been evoked in any passing trichologist given a close-up sighting of his hair. The latter, dense, curly and of a peculiarly matt appearance, was hand cut, never washed, and rarely combed. It clung around his head with the tenacity of a virulent lichen.

"Oh mate," he greeted me warmly. "I seen you was home so I thought I'd just stop to see if I could put a bit of business your way, like." He presented me with a Gable smile and a Formby giggle.

"What's that, then?" I replied, not expecting anything of moment. But in that I was soon to discover, I was mistaken.

"Well," he continued. "I was down the Beaulieu Road Sales the other day an' I met Bilious Bill – you know, old Badger's son. Anyway he was with a lady, a very high-class woman, God knows how Bilious Bill got hold of her! Anyway she wants a waggon and horse, she fancies the gypsy life. Bill've already found her a waggon – off one of them Dowsetts over Netley way. But she's very fussy about what horse she buys, and by all accounts she knows a good un when she sees one."

Having been given this unexpected information, of seemingly just the sort of buyer that we had in mind, there seemed little point in not taking full advantage of it.

"When could she be persuaded to come and see the mare, Gilly? I enquired. He grinned in his Formby mode. "Well I 'spects she'd have to come over with Bilious –cos he'd expect something out of the deal, for his time an' that."

"And you," I observed.

"Well, I'd deserve a drink, wouldn't I? Bringin' you together, like – on'y fair as I sees it."

"What do you call a drink?" I asked.

His Gable expression to the fore he looked hard at me. "I should have to have a fiver – at the least."

"And another from Bilious, I suppose," I presumed. All things considered, however, it might be well worth it, or so I hoped.

"I'll tell you what," he replied. "I'll 'phone up Bilious tonight from a call box and try to get him over here – maybe Saturday or Sunday, if you'll be here"

I agreed to this suggestion and he prepared to leave.

"That Bilious ain't a bad old boy – he'll play fair with us so long as we plays fair by him. I've had a few deals with him so I knows what I'm on about."

With these words of comfort he entered the over-loaded little van which, after a hesitant start, and emission of much blue smoke, eventually transported him away.

True to his word he stopped by the next day and assured me that Bilious Bill and the lady, a Mrs. Pringle-Harris, might be expected on the Saturday afternoon at about two o'clock. It was only two days ahead.

At that point our feelings were very mixed, but the decision was made, and everything appeared to be pointing in the right direction.

Saturday morning dawned, a beautiful autumn day. I jumped down from the waggon and lit the fire from a bundle of wood I had gathered the night before, as was customary. The black kettle was soon boiling and the tea was made, whilst I hung the hoop-handled iron frying pay from the kettle-crane and fried some bacon and mushrooms. Beshlie joined me, Nailer the Alsatian looking-on expectantly. We both agreed that Mrs Pringle-Harris *sounded* just the kind of buyer that we had hoped to discover. We could but wait.

In fact, almost on the appointed hour we perceived a smart capacious horse-box draw up at the gate. It was a bull-nosed Bedford of some age but in immaculate condition, with a middle-aged female at the wheel. From the passenger side there alighted a man, whom I rightly surmised to be the inexplicably named Bilious Bill. He proceeded to open the gate and signalled the driver to follow him.

"Mind them ditches, Mrs Pringle-Harris – we don't want the old motor to go arse over tit, s'know, Mrs Pringle-Harris," he called encouragingly to the driver.

He was an unattractive person, of middle-age and height, wearing old stained trousers, a blackish waistcoat and collarless shirt, the latter enlivened by a red and white spotted handkerchief around his neck. His eyes were pale grey and his face heavily lined, with deep furrows across his brow and down each cheek. A half-smoked Woodbine hung from his lower lip, whilst across the crown of his apparently bald head there stretched a moth-eaten cloth cap – its peak pulled downwards whilst its crown slunk backwards to the nape of his hairless neck. He walked with a forward-leaning, slightly ape-like gait, expectorating at every few paces. He was not a man to whom I felt in any way drawn. He lacked the faintly eccentric charm of Gilly Gayle. The horse-box drew up and a portly gentlewoman of indeterminate age or temperament descended.

"Mrs Pringle-Harris?" I enquired, rather unnecessarily, and introduced myself.

Wearing an all-enveloping oil-cloth jacket, despite the warm weather, off-white jodphurs and riding boots, her equestrian leanings were unmistakeable. We walked across the field to where Whitefeet was grazing, attached to a long 'plug-chain.' This I had done purposely in order to show that she was used to being tethered, a vital necessity for any Travellers' horses when roadside verges or old commons are their temporary grazing places. She raised her head at our approach, striking a flattering pose.

"What a lovely neck she has," observed Mrs Pringle-Harris, in the refined yet throaty tones often encountered in those of her background.

"Yes," I agreed, adding, "and being a Welsh cob she is a really good doer – in fact, it's wise to keep her tethered in the summer otherwise she'll eat herself fat."

"I know what you mean, Mr Reeve," agreed Mrs Pringle-Harris with unbending formality.

Bilious Bill stood in the background, looking non-committal, smoking and spitting in turn.

As I had been told, she was without doubt knowledgeable about horses, and examined Whitefeet in the minutest detail, seemingly finding no fault. She hinted that she would like to see the waggon being pulled – which was not entirely unreasonable. However, I showed her some photographs of the turnout on the roads, both lanes and main thoroughfares, which seemed to satisfy her.

We had by then been joined by the insanitary figure of Gilly Gayle, whose odour that day permeated even through the clouds of cigarette smoke surrounding Bilious Bill. He was fresh from the rubbish dump.

"Oh madam, you couldn't fault that mare – she'd pull a waggon with all four wheels locked," he announced, hoping to please.

"Well, I don't think we should want her to do a cruel thing like that," rejoined Mrs Pringle-Harris, gazing with some disgust at the dishevelled speaker. "What do you think, Bill?" she enquired of the poker-faced Bilious, who flickered a glance in my direction at which I winked back at him.

"She doesn't seem too bad at all, Mrs Pringle-Harris," answered the king-pin in the possible deal. "Good sort've a working mare by all accounts I should say."

In those far-off days waggon-horses were priced amongst Travellers at anywhere from £40 to £100 at most. In view of the 'drinks' to be deducted I knew that I would have to extract a price around the top end of the market.

"So, upon being asked to name a price I answered straight-facedly, "Well, I can honestly say she's the best waggon horse I've ever owned – and plenty of years left in her. *And* I can warranty her as quiet and perfect on the roads in traffic. You'd be hard put to find a better one. Anyway I want £110 for her if you want her."

I knew that Bilious Bill would, as the lady's agent as it were, make a token attempt to get me to reduce my price. It was all part of the unspoken agreement. She repeated her question to him:

"What do you think, Bill?"

"I tell you what, Mrs Pringle-Harris," he replied, giving me a distant glance, "I thinks he's a bit too steep for that mare," he continued.

"She's a *good* horse, Madam, I can promise you that – wuth every penny of what the man's asking," pronounced Gilly, luckily standing some feet away. At that Bilious Bill drew the possible buyer to one side and whispered words of advice in her ear. She responded to his confabulations by turning towards me and issuing an offer:

"I'm afraid I wouldn't be willing to pay that amount, Mr Reeve," she said, "very nice mare that she is. But I would give you £80."

It was my turn then. "I'm sorry, I couldn't let her go for that," I replied sadly. Then a thought struck me.

"But what I will do is this: I'll take £95 for the mare and throw in the set of white-metal harness that is hers – and that's a really good offer." A further conferment ensued, in quiet tones with nodding of heads. Mrs Pringle-Harris eventually confronted me.

"Well, I think we can do a deal at that, Mr Reeve," she acknowledged, smiling faintly.

It was scarcely the most exciting deal of my experience, perhaps a little too civilized, but in most of its returns it was all I could have wished for. I knew that Whitefeet would be going to a genuine horse-lover, and that there was no danger of her ending up in the glue factory or of being exported to the Continent for human consumption.

My confidence in Mrs Pringle-Harris was in no way lessened when she beckoned me to the cab of the horse-box and withdrew the requisite payment from a leather brief-case.

Indeed it was no more than a quarter of an hour before the mare was led into the box and they were off – not before I had managed to secrete a five-pound note in the palm of Bilious Bill when the attention of Mrs Pringle-Harris was momentarily diverted. Almost inaudibly he grunted his appreciation. Soon they were gone, the sweet-sounding Bedford engine resounding up the lane and into the distance.

Gilly, who had not left, peered expectantly at me. Thus he too was the recipient of a £5 note, which he accepted with considerable grace – his Formby side coming into full play. Both Beshlie and I felt a little mournful as such an important part of our recent past slipped out of sound and view: it was our last contact with the horse-drawn life.

After the departure of Gilly Gayle I built up the *yog* (fire) and Beshlie set about preparing us a fine stew with the addition of a multiplicity of vegetables and herbs. Rabbits were still welcome food as the area had not then been overtaken by myxomatosis – a horrific disease, which tended to make the little animals less welcome fare to all but the most insensitive of eaters. Despite our feelings of loss and trepidation we were still able to enjoy its tastefulness.

On the occasions when we stopped in the field at Fryern Court, Dorelia, the long-time second 'wife' of Augustus, generously encouraged us to help ourselves from the variety of produce still flourishing in undisciplined abundance in the large, if untended, garden. It was situated, almost out of sight, beyond the more formal and exotic layout within the shadow of the house, the occupants of which, when glancing out of the windows, would be appeased by its splendour. There were urns, busts on plinths, and Grecian statues in playful poses – also two lily-ponds each situated in its own little sunken space,

29

bordered by flag-stone foot paths for romantics to tread should they wish to study the flora closely.

Alas, however, only one of the ponds was still so stocked. The other, for no accountable reason that I could fathom, had become inundated by the presence of myriad black-water snails, so numerous that no vegetation was to be seen. Their profusion was beyond comprehension – poor creatures marooned in a congregation of their own making, apparently unaware of the sanctuary of the other pond so little distance away.

A few years later I witnessed a similar situation in a miniature lake in front of a large suburban villa in an opulent part of Surrey. Though in that case frogs were in place of snails, but in almost equal numbers, and distinctly more dramatic in their behaviour. The whole surface was pulsating in alarming unison, whilst an opera of croaking was more that audible, even to the aurally disadvantaged.

The occasion was possibly made more memorable to me by the utterance of the property owner's elderly gardener, who caught me staring wistfully at the spectacle.

"Ar, look at 'em," he mused. "Fuckin' theirselves to death, I shouldn't wonder!" Such is nature, appreciated by the unlikeliest of persons.

On most evenings between the hours of six and eight Augustus would receive visitors in his study – some welcome, others not so. Wherein, seated at a large table, with several bottles of red wine, and invariably a box of a hundred Woodbine cigarettes, he would be host to a variety of people. At times, however, his temper could become uncertain if he found himself in the company of boring or uninteresting people. Should that be the case he would either dismiss them fairly curtly, or alternatively would switch-off his hearing aid unobtrusively, thus allowing himself to sink into a private reverie.

I recollect one instance that caused me some mirth.

A rather loud-voiced woman of obvious social and artistic pretension was seated opposite Augustus and was, I could detect, causing him some irritation. Her wiry reddish blonde hair was bullied into submission by a pink ribbon, and her freckled features shone unashamedly in the evening light. The top half of her body, was mammiferously fighting a winning battle against the constraints of the frail buttoning of a yellow nylon blouse. Alas, on the downward gradient of the hill of life, she was of no great attraction. Her talk was not enlivened by humour or insight and I could see that it irritated her victim.

Augustus regarding her coldly from behind a newly acquired pair of exceptionally heavy-framed spectacles, lurking perilously towards the end of his nose. Apparently noticing them for the first time the rapacious woman exclaimed:

"Oh Gus, I *love* your glasses – aren't they wonderful!"

Eyeing her coldly the artist delivered the magnificent rejoinder:

"Well, I find they come in useful for scraping the duck-shit off the doorstep!"

In retrospect I find it curious to recall one or two rather demeaning occurrences at Fryern in which I became involved by the purest of accidents.

One such concerned a young Sicilian, when he had not long been employed at Fryern in the capacity of General Houseboy, engaged in the hope that his assistance would aid the flagging energies of Dorelia. His name was Mario, olive-skinned, black-haired, impassive of visage and aged nineteen. To add to the foregoing qualities he was able to boast of a complete ignorance of the English language. His association and communication was a combination of pantomime and merely mime. I had had no contact with him at all.

In any event early one morning I went across the field intending to pick some runner beans for us. By chance I decided to take a short-cut through the formal area beside the house. As I was passing the snailless sunken pond I sensed a movement to my left, where a small semi-concealed patio lay – a splendid sun-dial at its centre. Being curious at the unexpected movement I turned toward it and was not a little astonished at what met my eyes. For there squatted the white-jacketed figure of Mario in the process of answering the full call of nature in no limited fashion. Casting my gaze about him I saw, with even greater surprise, small heaps of human waste deposited in fetching patterns about the patio: obviously the result of some weeks' works!

Our surprise was mutual, though his appeared to be mixed with alarm. Hastily drawing up his black trousers he fled from the scene! Reflecting upon the situation, and its complications, I felt certain that, should some unsuspecting guest at the house discover this alimentary treasure-trove, all hell might break loose. Undoubtedly logic would point to me as the culprit!

Thus I realised what had to be done. It is to the credit of Dorelia that when I related my experience to her she remained calm and almost unmoved. She pointed out to me that Mario was from a very rural and backward area in which flush lavatories and even running-water was not part of their lives. Looking back I suppose one could not be have a fleeting admiration of the tenacity of this rural peasant in maintaining

31

the standards of family tradition. And who but the Johns could have failed to have been appalled by his behaviour? Strangely enough scarcely a week had passed before I found myself in an almost parallel situation.

I should mention that we had positioned our waggon close against an expanse of close-growing shrubbery which ran along the roadside to a depth of some fifteen or twenty feet, separated from both the roadside and the field by low iron fencing. This shrubbery provided a ready supply of dead wood for our fire, and an ideal avenue for privacy.

Sensible as I was to the remarks of an aged Welsh Traveller, who observed of the conditions prevailing on a common infested by 'rough' Travellers: "Well, aye man, God kill me, you never seen nothin' like it – all round the edges the ground was covered in discreeta!" Hence, armed with a shovel I was careful not to follow the pattern of the young Italian.

Alas, however, even such unremittingly scrupulous behaviour did not go without repercussions.

Seated by the fire, frying some bacon, I was suddenly alerted by the barking of our dog, luckily chained to a waggon wheel. I perceived the stalwart figure of a helmeted police constable pushing his bicycle towards us. He was nearing retirement age, with a rather uncertain expression on his face.

"Mr Reeves?" he enquired.

"Yes," I replied, a little surprised that he almost knew my name.

"Well, I'm afraid we've had a complaint from a lady….." he faltered.

"What about?" I asked, still mystified.

"It's about….. well in the bushes, like….she *saw* you…." he hesitated, unsure of how to proceed.

"*Saw* me?" I innocently replied, although by then I had begun to realise the implications.

"She says……" he hesitated once more, "you was going to the lavatory."

Refinement had triumphed. My instinct told me that the only course of action was for me to resort to an unimpeachable lie. I denied the possibility of such an incident. This resulted in something of an impasse, and the constable left, in a mood of slightly wavering uncertainty.

To some, perhaps, the rarefied atmosphere of Fryern could have been slightly tainted by such biological experiences. Not for me, however; I decided to rise above it!

Chapter 2

A Bit of Company

One evening I ascertained from the graceful and majestic Dorelia that no guests were expected – hence my visit would cause no interruption.

When I arrived at his study at soon after six o'clock the great man was seated at the table, a glass of wine in hand, puffing contentedly on a Woodbine. As only a spasmodic smoker myself in those days I was able to perceive its destructive powers.

"*Besh akai* (sit here)," he said, indicating a chair, "and have some wine."

After a fairly desultory conversation Augustus informed me that he had just heard from Miss Dora Yates, the then president of the Gypsy Lore Society, comprising an august body of scholars, in Liverpool. With a remarkable fluency in Romani, including the archaic 'Deep,' or 'inflected' dialect, Augustus John was an esteemed member. He had also been a friend of the late Romani man, 'Daisy' Lee, whose family had become almost Liverpool-bound. The purpose of the letter was to state that the middle-aged son of 'Daisy' would deem it a great honour to meet the famous 'Romani Rai' of whom his father had so often spoken. It was suggested that he, Clifford Lee, might journey from their bungalow in a suburb of Liverpool, accompanied by his wife, two young daughters, and his eighteen years old son. They proposed to undertake the journey with a touring trailer-caravan, pulled by their Commer van. Augustus seemed quite happy for them to come and stay in the same field as ourselves. In my experience the north-country Lees have almost all been very sociable, and invariably handsome in a Romani-featured way. The next day I was surprised that telephonic communication had ensued the previous evening, and that they were intending to arrive within two days, on the Saturday.

As the distance from Liverpool to Fordingbridge was considerable I did not imagine that they could appear before the afternoon. In fact, it was barely three o'clock on Saturday afternoon when I became aware of their equipage drawing-up at the gate.

Their turnout consisted of a Commer 25cwt van, a few years old, hand-painted in discreet tones of nut-brown and beige; whilst the trailer-caravan, a 12ft Thompson, was in similar hues. Only to the initiated would it have been instantly apparent that they belonged to Travellers.

A youth jumped out and swung the gate open whilst the van's engine revved enthusiastically for a comparatively small horse-power as it hauled the little trailer up the slight gradient into the field. Clifford Lee was a thin-faced, dark complexioned man, unmistakeably a Lee.

Once inside the field he climbed out of the cab and greeted me with a handshake, in a firmly-rooted 'Scouse' accent. Dressed in a light-coloured gabardine jacket, dark open-necked shirt, and black trousers, he did not appear to have been attracted to any of the more obviously Romani fashions of the time – which was a slight disappointment to me.

His wife, a frizzy-haired, faintly terrier-like Irish woman, not a Traveller, emerged from the van with two girls, both on the brink of their teens. One followed her father's colouration, whilst the other was red-haired and white-skinned: neither carried the Romani 'look.'

The son, however, resembled his father in every way more than his sisters did. (He was later, to his father's pride, to attend university and devote himself to the academic life, whilst in no way denying his *posh rat* [half-blood] status.) They decided to stop not far inside the gate, some twenty yards from us. Soon they were setting about establishing themselves, and preparing a meal after their long journey. I was pleased to see that they gathered dead wood from the hedge and lit a *yog* (fire). I was also pleased to see that they had a *chitty* (tri-pod) from which hung a well-used black cooking pot. In that respect I warmed to them.

A little later Clifford sauntered over to our fire, followed by his son, and we exchanged 'credentials.' In which exercise, of course, the discovering of mutual friends and acquaintances was of the utmost importance. It was a little disappointing for me that Clifford had married 'out' – which I was later told, his father had also done. I found that Clifford, although ostensibly likeable, would appear to be living in a faintly confusing manner.

The fact that he seemed pleased to be able to tell me that he regularly socialised with officers working in Liverpool's most notorious prison was enough to offend my sensibilities. One could not help but feel that the line had been crossed. There are, after all, certain occupations which conjure up no feeling other than distaste or mild nausea.

As far as I could gather from our conversation he earned his living by calling door-to-door offering his services as a Grinder – of knives, shears, lawnmowers, or indeed any metal objects which would benefit from being sharpened.

It was, I found out, a surprisingly well remunerated profession if accompanied by an unremittingly technical sales technique. I can call to mind a Traveller who, over the course of forty years, starting out with a home-made push-barrow, later advancing to a motor van and a mechanical grinder, prospered to an astonishing degree – eventually entering the tarmacadam business in a large way of trade, specialising in car-parks, private drives and roads. His success was so great that he retired in his early fifties, spending the remainder of his days in Spain. His dreams had come true. And who are we to question them?

I had but recently discovered, by chance, that the faintly nefarious Gilly Gayle was employing someone on a part-time basis, he told me, who was engaged for the purpose of assisting in the sorting-out of the uncontrolled mounds of 'stock' which, owing to Gilly's exertions, were accumulating at an alarming rate.

It was apparent, even to the untutored onlooker, that it was a task that would assuredly stretch ahead indefinitely. If viewed impersonally it seemed beyond the realms of possibility that such bulk could have been accrued over so little time by one single man and his Ford 8 van: it was, undoubtedly a tribute to the stamina of both.

Walking past the property, grandly described by Gilly as his "house and yard" I espied a matt and dirt-caked being, scraping and raking among a malodourous unidentifiable rubbish heap, a small cigarette dangling from his mouth. Instinctively sensing my presence as I was passing he raised a blackened hand in salute.

Even from beneath his coating of grime there was an indefinable energy about him. I stopped and he approached me: he was of no great height, unimpressive in stature. He was bald-headed, with a ring of pitch black hair around the back and sides of his starved-looking face, with eyes of a glittering black intensity – like those of a field-mouse.

He was, I could discern, a Romani man. Upon that basis I began a conversation with him: he without doubt delighted to have a conversation with a person with at least some fellow-feeling. We talked for nearly half an hour. As happens in the strange coincidences of life our paths would cross on several occasions following that chance meeting.

I generally seemed to encounter him in Fordingbridge, to which little town he rode on an aged motor-cycle, attached, partly with wires, to a bullet-shaped sidecar, in which precarious cocoon a wan-looking pallid-faced *Gauji* (non-Romano) woman could sometimes be glimpsed, crouching in apparent terror, being whisked around the environs of

Fordingbridge by the slightly unhinged Horace – who it turned out was a Lock, and had met Clifford during one of his sojourns in Liverpool in his more prosperous times. How he had ever eventually wound up in the lowly position of being virtually a 'Dosser' for such socially disadvantaged a person as Gilly must be accepted as one of life's mysteries.

Indeed soon after the arrival of Clifford and his family at Fryern he was to be heard at the gate, motor-cycle revving and misfiring to an equal measure. I do not know who was the more surprised at their meeting so unexpectedly. I believe that they both appreciated it as being one of the coincidental happenings that not infrequently occur in the Traveller life-style. Should old *enemies* thus meet, of course, the results can be less pleasurable.

Even more astonishing perhaps was the fact that Horace immediately recognised the rather anonymous little Thompson trailer as having been at one time the property of an old Romani called Rabbi! He left after a short while, with promises that he would be over again during Clifford's stay.

"There's a state the man's in," observed Clifford when he had gone. "And him a proper Romani man too."

Apparent failure is no cause for celebration in the Travellers' life. On first meeting Horace I detected signs of a mentally off-balance personality, in which small events would be magnified in his eyes.

This was proved the following day when, with customary revs and back-firings Horace sped across the field at break-neck pace, skidding to a halt by Clifford's trailer. The Irish woman had built up a fire and hanging in the flames from a *chitty* was a black pot, the contents intended for their 'tea'

Clifford, myself, and Horace were lying on the grass a few yards from the fire when suddenly, without warning, Horace leapt up, several feet in the air, holding one wrist in apparent agony and screaming with pain.

"The Lord paralyse me – I been stung by de wopsie; it's killing me!"

Clifford and I reacted in slight shock at the antics being performed before us, endeavouring to reassure him. But he would have none of this despite our well intentions, and became almost hysterical when we suggested driving him to a doctor.

"No! No, man, No!" he cried. Adding for dramatic effect: "He'd give me needles, I know it......I can't stand no needles. My Blessed Lord I can't have no needles."

For added dramatic impact he flung himself to the ground, wallowing about in a mixture of pain and terror. Though, of course, in a person of so melodramatic a disposition, it was difficult to determine if either emotion was genuine or assumed.

"He's a fucking *dinilo* (fool), " I murmured to Clifford, with the sympathy of a youthful voyeur.

Clifford nodded, and we agreed to try to coax the by now lachrymose patient to lie still and rest, whilst the Irish woman applied some form of homemade medicament to the afflicted limb – which Horace received with faint moans of fear.

It was several hours later, after 'tea' that we drove his recumbent form back to Gilly's property, where the reception of his haggard and listless partner seemed to evoke little visible revival of his spirits.

Gilly was apparently out on one of his crepuscular refuse collections, so we were able to gaze uninterruptedly upon the fruits of his toils. In truth we viewed it with the incredulity of arrivals from another planet.

Since my last visitation the 'stock' had grown well over ten-fold in its accumulations. It had almost, as if by nature, begun to develop its own aesthetic art form: tunnels ran under some of the more bulky objects, whilst narrow footpaths ran between huge piles of tins and bottles, some leaning in defiance of natural law, others straight and handsomely constructed.

Everywhere there was something to look at, and to wonder at. Even the most jaded would have been mildly excited by such organised chaos. Like much of today's so-called Conceptual Art it had no value but was interesting to look at, if only for a short time.

It became obvious that Horace and his partner were not, as it were, house-guests in the shed that Gilly inhabited. Rather were they existing in a small and decaying shepherd's hut of about six-feet by eight, a mixture of corrugated iron and wood, on four stout little iron wheels to assist in its mobility when it was used at lambing-time by its original owner. It had a certain charm, though lacked any fittings designed to ameliorate the living conditions. Indeed, apart from a bed across the end, one small table, and a cupboard the only comfort was an old fire-stove – the chimney of which projected from the roof for two feet or more.

We managed to deposit the slightly shame-faced Horace on to the bed and departed as soon as possible.

Gilly's old Shepherd's Hut

As we reached home we were a little surprised to find a brand-new Humber Hawk Estate parked beside the field gate, a burly man seated inside. As we drew up I was able to see that it was the painter and sculptor Sven Berlin.

I had first met him a few years before, when he was encamped on the New Forest, not far from Lyndhurst, with his then wife Juanita and their baby son. Wishing, apparently, to escape from the bohemian life-style that they had embraced amongst the artists' colony at St. Ives in Cornwall, which had begun to pall, they embarked with a rather large Romani waggon which needed a big and powerful horse to pull it. They further augmented their possessions in the form of a smaller piebald horse and a trap. There was no doubt that they made a striking sight.

Sven himself was in his early forties, of the kind of physique sported by circus strong-men and adagio-dancers. Perhaps not surprising in view of the fact that he was able to boast of spells in both such callings before, one presumes, he had made his presence felt in more aesthetic circles.

Juanita, his second and recent wife, was a much smaller figure. With long and thick black hair and eyebrow-baiting fringe, a well-shaped face and dark of eye, she was hard to define. She proved to be a curious mixture of both the horsey and the 'arty-crafty' – with a touch of stage-gypsy in her apparel. By and large they were a pleasure to behold. However, after a spell in their waggon near Lyndhurst they found refuge on the land of a sympathetic woman who gave them somewhere to stay. Fortune appeared to smile on them when, to the astonishment of those who knew them, Juanita became the beneficiary of a relative's will – the fulsome amount of which, apparently, enabled them to purchase a large farmhouse and grounds in one of the most attractive areas of the New Forest.

I only undertook one visit to the property, during which I was plentifully astonished – nay overawed – by its opulence and splendour of fittings and equipment, including an immense kiln in which, I was told, Sven was able to cast his sculptures in bronze! I was duly impressed. For a man whom I had heard described as, "A First-class Second-class Artist," fortune had indeed smiled.

It transpired that he was, for a few days, host to a Swedish film-star of that era, Mai Zetterling. The latter had expressed a fervent desire to meet Augustus John and it had been arranged for the following Wednesday evening.

Hoping further to impress the film star Sven asked if he could bring her over to meet our little gathering in the field after she had met Augustus. I could see that Clifford (fresh from the social whirl of Maghull) was taken by the idea, so it was agreed that we might perform the rites of hospitality on a fairly grand scale by our standards. Sven suggested that he might bring Juanita and, oddly to my mind, his two grown-up children from his first marriage, Paul and Janet. As an added ingredient I suggested to Clifford that we invite Horace, to add a touch of the unexpected perhaps. Beshlie, anti-social to the last, was shocked by the whole proceeding, but reluctantly agreed to appear.

With no current income, and the pressures of imminent motorisation and all its complications, my mind was not really in socialising mood.

39

The proposed visitation was not to take place for two days, so Beshlie and I set to work on the Bedford van. We had decided to convert the back, temporarily, into living accommodation of the simplest kind, in order that we could make an exploration into parts of Somerset hitherto unknown to us: it was planned as something akin to a holiday; a state that we had not experienced in all our time together. Beshlie has faith in her own adage: the world is divided into Makers and Breakers. Hence, as a member of the last category, I felt that it would not be expected of me to assist in the modifications of the van's interior. Disaster would have been the only result. Armed with a list, however, I was able to obtain at least some of the appendages that, I was told, were required.

Clifford, although supposedly being on a kind of holiday himself, insisted in 'going out,' accompanied by his son, each morning, with his grinder. With the aim of a little money-earning each day they were still maintaining the old-fashioned Traveller tradition – a tradition to which I adhere to this day. (I remember an elderly Traveller man summing up the philosophy well and neatly. "A bit of *moro* (bread), a bit of *minge* ('sex'), an' a bit of *loover* (money)! What more can you want?")

The Irish woman and the two girls tended to go out shopping in Fordingbridge, so our peace was largely undisturbed, and the grand conversion could commence. On the first of their morning ventures Clifford and his son tried their luck in the immediate surroundings of Fordingbridge: not a locality that would have taken my fancy.

Upon returning home at about midday, and apparently after two or three hours of strenuous 'calling' their success had been minimal; indeed it would seem that almost every denizen of the little town had purged their spleen upon the unfortunate pair, dismissing them unceremoniously from their doorsteps. Only one resident, a person in declining years, had allowed them the privilege of bringing back to life a rust-infested lawnmower of a vintage and design seldom encountered even then. Alas, however, even their best efforts had failed to return the mower to the pristine condition expected by its irate owner.

To these sturdy Liverpudlians, their native wit and jollity to the fore, the morose and undemonstrative southerners seemed both sour and unresponsive. Undeterred, nonetheless, they vowed to widen their scope, promising to try next day the exalted surroundings of the City of Salisbury, trusting that in such religious climes their services would be more readily appreciated. There is, in the Travellers' world, no alternative to optimism.

As our waggon was situated in a more secluded position than the trailer of the Lees, it was decided that we would hold the gathering

40

within its shadow and that we would build up a larger than usual *yog*. Indeed for that purpose we hauled a considerable amount of dead wood from the bordering hedgerow and shrubs, laying it in readiness a few yards away from the fire-place.

We had no means to determine the atmosphere that might ensue: one presumed that, after visiting Augustus, their spirits, if flagging must be revived after the consumption of red wine at his table. Lest they might, however, arrive in a mournful condition, Clifford and I drove in his van to Fordingbridge and picked up a few cases of both light and brown ales and ten bottles of Guiness: it was polite to cater for all tastes!

We noticed the sleek Humber Estate, tastefully two-toned in the fashion of the era, glide quietly up to the house at about half-past six, presuming that its occupants would arrive at our fireside at about eight-o-clock or thereabouts.

This, in fact, was the case and we caught sight of them walking across the field as the light was beginning to fade. There appeared to be five or six figures discernible in the twilight. We had already piled the fire high with wood, pyramid style, and it was flaming readily in the evening air. All the Lees, Beshlie and myself were seated around it on a variety of low stools, upturned buckets, and old petrol tins: each with a cushion of sorts upon it. Just before sighting the approaching figures, our attention was diverted by the arrival of Horace on his motor-cycle combination, the silver-coloured side-car rolling dangerously, at war with its moorings.

He surged across the field at an unwise speed in the increasing darkness, without the advantage of a functioning headlight beam to illuminate his progress, nor any sort of lighting at the rear. Experience had proved to me that even in daylight any journey with him was a severe trial upon the nervous system of a passenger, whether riding aboard the machine, clinging to the back of Horace, or, seemingly even more hazardous, lying inside of the bullet-shaped sarcophagus that was the side-car. A single journey in the latter has remained in my memory, retained with some disrelish as being a very low point in my life. These were the days before it was compulsory for motor-cyclists to wear crash-helmets: before they became, by and large, a somewhat disfavoured breed of road users. As a bizarre alternative Horace had procured a rather unexpected form of headgear of the sort favoured by Sherlock Holmes; it had once been a bright check, but had been reduced by its then owner to an oil and dirt-stained dullness. It seemed a little uneasy at being swathed around his pinched and sallow features – a far cry from the upper-class noble deerstalkers of the Scottish

Highlands, let alone the great literary detective. Nonetheless it must be admitted that its incongruity was perhaps its interest.

Dismounting from the morose motor-cycle he left it clicking and gurgling to itself.

"How much is the tax on the bike?" enquired Clifford innocently.

"Dunno," replied Horace with a grin. "She runs just as well without it!"

That was possibly the only amusing remark that I ever heard from him. Darkness was falling rapidly and we made our way to the fire. By the time that the other visitors drew near we were only able to see them in its glimmering light.

Sven, too bulky to miss, arrived first, followed closely by the rather exotic Juanita, and his youthful son and daughter – her step-children. They were just in front of the film-star and her friend, to whom I was introduced by Sven with considerable affability. The only other film actress, who I met but briefly, was the truly wonderful Dianna Dors, who seemed to me, in my youthful admiration, to epitomise all that was magical in her world: the sight of her mammiferous embonpoint and flowing blonde hair, zooming through the streets of Virginia Water in her open-topped powder-blue Rolls Royce was enough to gladden the heart of anyone whose spirits had not been dulled by any form of suburban puritanism.

Strangely enough this film-actress, nay *star*, did not seem to exude any of the qualities of vitality or charisma that one might surely have expected to be the essentials of her profession; not that she was ungracious or impolite in any way. Sadly I must confess to remembering her name but not her face! Her friend, in the unforgiving light of the *yog*, showed up as a not unattractive young man, handsome enough in a Scandinavian pattern; his name eludes me after well over fifty years.

We managed to seat almost all of us around the glowing fireside, just the tall young Paul Berlin, and Clifford's son, were forced to stand in the shadows.

In the hopes of bringing some atmosphere to the gathering I had persuaded Beshlie to play her accordion. Her self-taught musical talent on the melodeon (or 'button accordion') has been applauded around Travellers' *yogs* in various parts of the country. One of my fondest memories is of the many times when she played duets with a renowned exponent of the instrument named 'Scotch Tom,' a middle-aged Traveller with whom we travelled considerably over the years in varying locations from Yorkshire to Cornwall and all around the South Coast.

He dealt in gold and jewellery and, as was his eldest son, was well-respected in the business. Even in Hatton Garden he was known as an astute dealer: it was just him and his eldest son. His other children did not follow the same path. Scotch Tom was, by choice, a long-distance Traveller who roamed wherever his fancy took him, preferring to stop on roadsides and disused patches of wasteland rather than endure the regimentation of Council Sites. Alas, however, in his last few years he was induced to sacrifice his freedom and become a resident on a newly-constructed Council Site in Surrey. It is a source of some sadness for me to realise that all of such old-fashioned and independent-minded Travellers have been lured from the roads – by persecution and misplaced good-intentions in equal measure. Both adding up to the same result.

I had tied the Alsatian a little distance away from the waggon, out of respect for the sensibilities of the guests, whose enjoyment may well have been curtailed by his unfriendly attitude. In the gloom I could just distinguish his silhouette as he viewed the scene with the suspicion of his breed.

As time went on, and our consumption of beer began to take hold, the atmosphere lightened to some extent. But, apart from the melodeon-playing, there were no natural entertainers capable of holding us in thrall by their singing, as always occurs at strictly Travellers' parties. The gaps between us were insurmountable; the inhibitions would not fall away. Hence, although the mood was amiable enough it did not ascend to the dizzy heights of irresponsibility that was really demanded on the night.

My own peace of mind was somewhat disturbed by Horace, who sitting beside me and more than a little tipsy, refused to refrain from expressing lascivious comments regarding the voluptuous thighs of Janet who was seated close by. His fascination was inordinate, and he became fanciful as to the possibility of his exploring their contours more thoroughly. In view of the company and their inevitable reactions I strongly advised him to keep such thoughts to himself. Although, as I gradually realised, he was convinced that he possessed all the seductive powers of a youthful Adonis it seemed that it was a view unlikely to be shared by any but the most retarded.

"She'd just tell you to fuck off!" I warned him, in as sympathetic mood as I could muster.

To my relief he relapsed into a kind of stupor and I winked at Clifford for sympathy. He, however, socialiser to the last, was away in earnest conversation with Sven and the slightly wilting film-star.

It was with some relief to me when they decided that the hour of departure had arrived, even Clifford showed signs of fatigue. In a short space of time I found myself alone, Beshlie too had retreated to bed. I sat gazing into the embers of the *yog*, managing to extract a couple of charred roast potatoes that were left. I munched on their charcoal texture with some pleasure, assisted by the beneficial effect of half a bottle of Guiness which I detected in the shadows. It had not, I decided, been a greatly successful event. Its curiosity value could only lay in the fact that those present failed dismally in the formation of a cohesive whole. Syncretism failed in the face of the unspoken tenets of the 'birds of a feather' condition. None seemed able to vacate their positions with ease: it was a minuscule picture of the larger society. Willing but incapable.

The next morning it had been arranged that Augustus was to have Clifford sitting for him, as he wished to execute a chalk-drawing of the very Romani –looking model. The drawing was completed in two sittings, Clifford posing in a straw-hat, light in colour and a pleasing contrast to his swarthy complexion. The subject was, to his astonishment, presented with a hundred pounds for the exercise: in those days no mean amount.

Upon the following day the Lees prepared to leave, fulsome in their praise of all that had occurred during their stay. Their only disappointment, surprisingly, was their contact with New Forest Travellers, whose repressed and ostensibly poverty-stricken accommodation seemed to jar against their own faintly respectable attitudes.

We watched as they left, unsure whether or not our paths might cross in the future: in fact, they did not, and could not do so now as Clifford is no longer with us, having passed on some years ago at no advanced age. (Sven Berlin too left this planet a few years ago; and Juanita expired but recently, having survived to the age of eight-six, dying, I am told, in the mournful conditions afforded by 'sheltered accommodation' for the elderly. A fact that I would have preferred not to have learned.)

Chapter 3

The Maiden Voyage

Once Clifford Lee and his family had left, their small-engined Commer van ticking-over healthily in the morning air, and drawing them steadily through the gate, we set about loading our own van with our few possessions preparatory to moving out on our journey to Somerset, as planned. I wished to leave as soon as possible after Clifford as, Traveller-style, I felt gloomy at the prospect of being left behind, alone, in the field. I had arranged with Augustus that we would return after no great length of time, in order that he could continue his pictorial records of Beshlie. Our great hope was that, in our absence, he would not feel dissatisfied with his work and, as was his habit in later years, discard it in favour of starting anew.

We locked up the waggon, leaving it stationed in the lee of the hedge, out of sight of the road.

The Bedford was, even with our very few personal possessions, well-loaded with dog-kennel, bantam-house, and bird cage – none of which was visible from the driver's cab as it was separated, in the manner of all much models, known as 'box-vans.'

We decided as first-time motorists, as well as virgin holiday-makers, to meander slightly in our journey towards Somerset. With that in mind I thought to make a first stop near Weymouth in Dorset, aiming for an old-fashioned Travellers' stopping-place at 'Culliver's Tree.' The latter was a slightly barren piece of land, from which lofty heights it was possible to gaze down upon the sea. It was in an area of Dorset as yet unspoilt. In those days, of course, it still possessed a charm and beauty of its own, and horse-drawn vehicles belonging to both Travellers and farmers were no unusual sight.

The Bedford was petrol-driven and, experience taught us, would travel about fifteen miles on a gallon: it was to be another ten years before diesel engines were adopted, almost universally, for even small commercial vehicles. The noise, smell, and poor performance of the early diesel engines were such that they offered little temptation to the average driver unless, perhaps, aurally handicapped.

Eventually our loading-up, or 'packing-down,' was complete and our first long-distance journey by horse-power, as opposed to horse, was about to commence. In some ways it was achievement in its finest hour.

I had taken the precaution of putting twelve gallons into the fuel tank – and was heartened to receive a comforting amount of change from the five-pound note I offered in payment. To my relief the van started without hesitation, without the use of the maligned choke, and we were off, out on to the road. We had youth, food, a certain amount of money, and unlimited optimism as our most valuable luggage.

To set off from Fordingbridge and head for Weymouth in Dorset might appear faintly eccentric to those for whom a direct route to their objective was the most reasonable. To me, however, it seemed a pleasurable choice, allowing us to follow familiar paths before casting ourselves into the fearsome territory of 'strange country.' How naïve that sounds today. Yet, even as late as the nineteen fifties, before mass foreign-travel, for a person to move their dwelling even as little distance as a hundred miles it could be as though going to a foreign land.

Indeed, I recently met a man who had committed a murder, quite justified in the circumstances, who in fear of the death penalty, (this was in the nineteen forties) abandoned his wife and child and fled to a neighbouring county. Apparently never dreaming of the possibility of him actually leaving the locality in which he was born the law cast no nets outside its boundary. In any event the man, whom I met when he was in his eighties, had soon struck up congruous relations with a young woman possessed of both physical and financial endowments and embarked on a new life, quite untroubled by his past, fathering two sons and three daughters, all apparently unaware of the quirks of their father, or the existence of a half-brother in the adjoining county of Dorset. The 'innocence' of such times will never be seen again. So it was that in a high spirit of adventure we sent out on our first experience in the luxury of motorised transportation.

It was not long before we had left Ringwood in Hampshire behind, by-passing it neatly, and heading in the direction of Poole in Dorset. This too we by-passed, taking the road towards Wareham. Upon so doing we soon became aware of the large sweeping area on our right hand side, known to Travellers as 'Poole Common.' It was then the refuge of enormous numbers of both waggons and trailers, the inhabitants of which relied on it as somewhere to stop, almost all belonging to the strata classed as 'old-fashioned' or 'rough Travellers' by their more successful brethren. They spread themselves across the barren heathland in little family groups in grand and attractive disarray. Some of the denizens thereon rarely vanished from its environs, whilst others, ourselves included, made only fleeting visits when in search of more refined stopping-places. Nearest to the actual roadside were what appeared to be the smarter trailers, all with newly painted lorries or vans to tow them. Most of the trailers had the additional comfort of a green square-framed tent standing beside them, used for cooking and other domestic purposes. They were of a design especially favoured by Travellers and which were made by a long-established firm in Somerset. With stout wooden frames and heavy-duty green canvas they were a little unwieldy: though once erected, and with the addition of a wood or coal-burning 'Queenie' stove, were warm and dry – protection against even the harshest of weather conditions. In later years their place became usurped by light-weight aluminium-framed versions, covered in coloured plastic – some even sporting floral patterns! More exotic, but less sturdy.

Kitchen Tent

As we drove past in the flow of traffic I noticed several people whom I knew, and they waved in salutation.

Behind these trailers and tents, stretching into the distance, were both waggons and more trailers; many of the latter being merely boxy little touring models which were not intended for permanent living. Without insulation or double-glazing their occupants found that keeping condensation and dampness at bay was almost a fulltime occupation. A few years on, of course, the construction of trailers improved greatly. Once it was realised that Travellers were a profitable market for 'luxury' trailers several enterprising firms commenced their production, gradually becoming more and more ornate and rococo – probably reaching their zenith in the form of the beautiful Vickers and Westmorland Stars, in the '70's and '80's.

There were coloured horses tethered here and there as far as the eye could see, and the smoke and scent from the wood-fires beside most of the homes infected the atmosphere with its characteristic odour, so familiar to me. That year, alas, public outcry became more vehement as numbers grew, despite the lack of *Gaujo* habitations nearby. The 'Ratepayers' demanded the eviction of the Travellers, even voiced through the medium of the local press, with the kind of malice and self-satisfied hatred which I have never seen being directed against any other minority or ethnic group: a form of abuse invariably generated by the 'unauthorised' presence of any Travellers who attempt any sort of settlement – either temporary or permanent.

Upon our reaching Wareham we drove on to a car park at the end of the town, adjoining the bank of the River Frome. It was an inviting scene, with boats of varying sizes moored beside a towpath, following the river.

We devoured a few sandwiches and allowed Nailer a certain amount of controlled freedom from the back of the van. Just as we had finished our simple fare we discerned the echoing sound of horses' hooves nearby, disclosing a fairly large black cob pulling a four-wheeled 'trolley' laden with 'light iron' scrap in the shape of sheets of rusting corrugated iron and disintegrating car bodies. Seated on the footboard, hunched and semi-comatose looking, was an aged Traveller man, dressed in a well-worn suit of 'Derby' tweed – a cloth once much favoured for its ability to provide warmth and insulation for its wearer in even the most demanding of weather. A black and white spotted neckerchief was a gesture to bygone fashions too, whilst an old velour hat pulled-down low on his brow, was of a darkness in tone that was almost matched by the deeply-lined features of the old man himself. Wispy tufts of snow-white hair protruded from beneath the hat in wondrous contrast. His eyes were cloudy-looking and rheumy, constantly in need of attention from the oleaginous piece of cloth with which he dabbed at them. I recognised him instantly as Old Siddy, by then in his late seventies. He was the oldest surviving offspring of the twenty-one children that his mother had born. In her nineties, at that time, she was still alive and was then in the company of one of her septuagenarian daughters and her family, still itinerant, if only in a limited area of Dorset. I had not seen her for a year or so, when she was on the move near Sturminster Newton with her daughter's family: three waggons in all. Driving her own waggon, with her old and trusted mare, she was indeed a wonder of nature, a sanguine memory to treasure.

Old Siddy drew his ageing black horse to a halt upon catching sight of me and smiled in recognition, dabbing vigorously at his left eye.

"How's you getting' on, my boy?" he enquired politely, turning his attention to his right eye.

"All right thank you Uncle Siddy," I replied, giving him the title, Traveller-style, out of respect for his age. "Still on the same place?"

"Ar, my boy," he said, adding mournfully: "I 'spects I shall bide there till they takes me out in me box."

"Oh dear, don't say that," I observed sympathetically. "How are you keeping?" Old Siddy gazed at me, evincing no improvement of spirits.

"I bin underneath two doctors – an' they gid me about ten tablets apiece – God's cuss they tablets." He watched for my reaction as I digested his plight.

"Me ole ticker's fucked," he continued gloomily. "Me *yoks* (eyes) is gone, an' I'm a-plagued wi' the screws."

He gave me every impression of believing himself to be at death's door. As I was acquainted with almost all of his brothers and sisters – who were spread around throughout Dorset, Wiltshire and Hampshire, I felt it polite to ask after them. It was a query that I should have omitted. Before I could prevent it he began to relate *their* health crises also.

"Johnny've had his leg took off – lyin' there in Poole Hospital an' lookin' like *mullerin'* (dying), Mary-Jaynet, me oldest sister, 'ave gone blind, an' Sonner've had three of his fingers bit off by an Irishman in the pub. Joe've got branchitees goin' on pneumonia, an' Half-Ear've bin put into hospital last week an' gie three weeks to live, wi' that complaint – you knows what I mean?"

His tale of family ailments would undoubtedly have continued, but when I had managed to apprise him of our destination, which seemed to him, as a horse-man, quite a long distance, he bade me farewell and wished me good luck.

One of his old sisters was already there with her family, and had been for a week or more.

"You can bide up there at Culliver's Tree 'til you'm grey-headed," Old Siddy had assured me, going on to remind me that I would not be sort of company as his sister Meena and her husband Eli had twelve children in all, most still with them. Only one son and a daughter had flown the nest. They ranged in age from four years to their late twenties. It had been a long-term breeding plan!

Old Siddy, as well as enjoying the honour of being the oldest survivor of the twenty-one brothers and sisters, was almost unique amongst them in so far as being settled-down on his own small piece of land not far from Wareham, living in a minute asbestos bungalow. Though beside the latter accommodation he also had a square-bowed 'open lot' waggon, kept, he told me, in case the fit to 'go away' travelling again overtook him. There was also a large barn, three-sided and rather a poor shelter against the elements. However, Old Siddy found it useful as a harbour for his collections of rags and non-ferrous metals before their sale. Several carts and trolleys, in varying condition, and two or three sets of driving harness enlivened the scene.

Since the death of his wife he resided mostly on his own, though at the time of my last visit he had been joined by his middle-aged daughter who was at odds with her husband and contemplating legal separation.

"God's cuss that man!" she had exclaimed to me. "'Fore this year's out he'll be a-getting' his rivorce papers. Like me dead mother I shain't bide 'long of 'ee no more."

It was not a course of action taken by many Travellers in those times.

Just before our farewells Old Siddy insisted on showing me, not for the first time, his 'Pass' with which he had been presented by the M.O.D. Upon the official document was a startling image of himself accompanied by an authorisation for him to collect unwanted scrap-iron from the Army Camp at Bovingdon. To achieve such a 'Pass,' I was proudly told, was the ambition of every scrap-man in the county; it was the key to acceptance and even mild prosperity. I could think of no one more deserving than the inscrutable recipient, whose un-displayed wealth was legendary to all his family.

We took the Wool road from Wareham, discovering it to be pleasantly little-used, and headed towards Weymouth in tranquil mood: it was but early afternoon and time was of our own.

As we ascended a sympathetic incline I changed gear from fourth to third with a confidence and deftness that surprised even myself, performing the intricacies of 'double de-clutching' with perfectly controlled revs and nimble footwork. At that period in motoring history, a so-called 'crash' gearbox was standard in almost all sizes of commercial vehicles. It was not until around 1950 that the delights of the 'synchromesh' gearboxes were absorbed into the manufacture of lorries and vans from the medium to largest sizes. From then on it was unnecessary to attune oneself to the former ramifications. (Heaters, then unknown, soon followed.)

However, once such an important practice being essential to the motor's well-being became obsolete, it was hard to abandon – although later, as a matter of course, even the most stubborn devotee did so.

After a while, admiring the purity of the Dorset countryside, we stopped at an old-fashioned looking village store, from whence we were able to obtain a lump of home-cured bacon, some potatoes, carrots, onions and cabbage and a cottage loaf of an individual shape. For added luxury we bought some bananas and a bag of oatmeal. Nourishment was our aim!

Dorset Victuals

Soon we were nearing the end of our journey, passing through amicably rural scenery, largely untroubled by the vindictive race of motorist who seems only too common on our roads today: all speed-mad as they hurtle past the more sedate drivers, horns blaring, and their pallid faces contorted with fury. We were, of course, unable to appreciate that we were experiencing what is called The Golden Age of

Motoring. Like so many other aspects of life it is only in retrospect that their qualities can be appreciated.

The last time that we had stopped at Culliver's Tree was with our horse and waggon, approaching it through narrow lanes. I decided to take the same route and as we approached the stopping-place, up a long hill-path, I was able to make out two waggons and a number of figures around them. Five or six horses, several coloured, were tethered on long 'plug chains' within view of the waggons. It was the kind of scene that, even in those days, was becoming rarer. With mighty revs I changed to second gear and we were soon almost level with the group.

Seeing a 30cwt Bedford they had realised that it was a Traveller van, and gazing enquiringly at it they relaxed when they recognised us. It was indeed the family of Eli and Meena, one of Old Siddy's sisters. There were two waggons, one for them and the other belonging to their married son Jobi and his wife and two small children.

We exchanged greetings warmly, and they made us feel welcome. They showed some surprise at our change of life-style, Eli and Meena expressing slight dubiosity as to the wisdom of our choice.

Young Jobi, however, was full of praise, expressing his hope of doing the same.

"You can't beat moties to get about wi' today. The old *grys* (horses) have had their day, *mush*. If I kin get hold've a *slang* (licence) I shall have meself one in a minute."

"Gaaan, boy – you'd never git through they testies," observed his father disparagingly.

"I tell you what," rejoined Jobi, slightly put out. "I'd gie a man a hundred pounds to go through the testy for me."

A hundred pounds in those days was a goodly sum, and hard to earn.

The opportunity so unexpectedly thrown my way to become a surrogate driver, as it were, for worthy and deserving cases seemed an enticing prospect: a source of income that I felt unable to deny myself in time to come. In these less forgiving times it would be impossible for the contemporary bureaucrat to realise the degree of freedom that the average person enjoyed. The phrase 'I.D.' had not been conceived; indeed so far as one's identity was concerned it was accepted without question or investigation. To live under any name one chose was a choice denied to nobody. For those who wished to indulge in a multi-persona existence few bars were placed in their way. Even the act of obtaining official documents presented no problems in relation to names or addresses to those who sought them.

There was about the waggons of both Eli and Jobi an air of decay and shabbiness, and even in the people too. The clothing of them all was donated from lowly origins. However, with an eye for style they had mostly managed to don a pleasing mixture of the conservative and the radical, with bold mismatching's of colour not shied away from. We stopped beside the waggon of Jobi and his wife Roseanne, and after gathering some wood from a nearby copse it was not long before the fire was burning well and our black pot, in which our meal was simmering, lurked above it, suspended from the kettle-iron. Beshlie joined me, having been engaged in conversation with Meena, with whom she was on friendly terms. Some of the younger children had been listening, slightly mesmerized.

"Come outa the 'oman's face – there's brazen *chavies* (children)!"

Meena had complained, not appreciating how well developed were their manners; different indeed to many suburban *Gaujo* children whose self-importance may have been encouraged to a point that they would think nothing of interrupting the conversation of adults when in full spate. Alas, it is sad for such children – only their parents could love them!

My intention was not to stay long, maybe only another day, at Weymouth before heading towards Somerset via the familiar country of Dorchester, Blandford, Shaftesbury, and from thence into areas with which we were unfamiliar.

The next day we were up early, the weather still promising with the indefinable magic of late summer on the brink of autumn. It was a time to be treasured by outdoor-dwellers more than those to whom the onset of winter occasions no more effort than the activation of the central-heating.

I had saved some wood from the night before so it was no time before the *yog* was blazing merrily and I had made tea, and fried a few rashers of the home-cured bacon. Before Beshlie had descended from the rear of the van I had even toasted some bread as well: there was little more that life could offer!

Eli, Meena and their children were all up and following the same course, tousle-headed and still sleepy-looking, around their fire. Their discourse, as ever, vigorous and dramatic, reverberated in the quiet morning light. Shouts, laughter and oaths issued forth in equal measure, uninhibited amongst themselves, safe in family unity mores.

"I thought you'd be a-led up in that *voodrus* (bed) for hours yet, young man," called Eli, laughing.

"*Kekker* (no)," I replied. "I like to be up and about – one hour in the morning's worth two in the afternoon."

They nodded in agreement, rinsing their faces from a single bowl of water, the men and boys combing it back through their unruly hair, preparing to go out 'calling.' Indeed two of the boys, Pincher and Lias, had soon harnessed-up a piebald pony and backed him into the shafts of a four-wheeled trolley. They were aiming to collect scrap-iron or rags; towards which goal they planned to spend the morning distributing leaflets to fortunate inhabitants in the locality of Weymouth.

The youth Pincher showed me one of the bills and I was delighted to see that it was one with which I was already familiar. It had about it an air of such archaic charm that I feel it is worth quoting in full, despite my having done so previously in my first book, *Smoke in the Lanes*.

The one he showed me was headed W. SMITH, under which was printed LICENCED DEALER, followed by an optimistic: 100 TONS OF OLD RAGS WANTED. CASH PAID. Then, in smaller print came the wondrous verses:

I beg with most respectful feeling,
Leave to inform you what I deal in:
I have not come your purse to try,
Yourself shall sell and I will buy.

So please look up that useless lumber,
Which long you may have left to slumber,
I'll buy old boots, old shoes, old socks,
Jackets, trousers, and smock frocks.

Towels, cloths, and cast-off linen,
Cords, cashmeres, and worn-out women's
Old gowns, caps, bonnets torn to tatters,
If fine or coarse it never matters.

Bed ticking, fustians, velveteens,
Stuffs, worsted cord and bombazines,
Old worn-out handkerchiefs and shawls,
Umbrellas and parasols.

Sheep netting, canvassing and carpeting,
Whatever else you have to bring:

And of the weight I'll soon convince you,
For which I pay the utmost value.

I'll purchase dirty fat, dusty bags,
Old roping, sacking, and old rags:
Both bottles, horsehair and old glass,
Old copper, pewter and old brass;
Old saucepans, boilers, copper kettles,
Pewters, spoons and other metals.

Old coins (not silver), ancient buttons,
Ladies' and gentlemen's left-off clothing,
Skins whether worn by hare or rabbit,
However small your stock, I'll have it.
I'll buy old rags, however rotten,
If made of woollen, hemp, or cotton.

I'll buy old iron cast or wrought,
And pay the money when 'tis bought.
If you have any bones to sell
Their value in a trice I'll tell.
So over your dwelling give a glance,
You never will have a better chance.

My price is good, my weight is just,
And mind I never ask for trust.
So just look up if but a handful,
And for the same I shall be grateful.

This notice will be called for in two hours'
time and I will take away all the old lumber
you may have.

"There's a *kushti* (good) bill, eh?" said Pincher, fishing for my approval.

"Best I've ever seen," I replied, not admitting that I had read it before.

"Me Uncle Joe writ it," announced Lias proudly. "He gid me dad five hundred of 'em in a deal they done."

"You gonna bide on yere today?" asked Pincher, who was the older brother. I told him of my plans, of which he seemed to agree. "Me brother Jobi's gettin' hisself a moty soon," remarked Lias.

"He'll have to git a *slang* fust, mind," reminded Pincher, adding hopefully: "I 'specs he'll find the right man to git one for him."

Oh the temptations that fall into one's lap!

"Well, we shall have to git on – this won't git the baby a new frock!" laughed Lias, and they set off at a good pace with a light-hearted optimism that one hoped would bring them just reward.

With our goldfinch mule singing from his cage hooked on the side of the Bedford, and the bantams scratching happily about on the edge of the fire, ours was indeed a picture of domestic bliss.

Meena and her two youngest children set off for a day in Weymouth, with some lace and 'lucky charms' as their means of extracting a few shillings from often antagonistic householders. In those times it was normal for a Romani woman to take at least one small child with her, sometimes even a baby in a 'sling' – partly as an inducement and partly as an education in the art of successful 'calling.' (How depressing it is to read that when Eastern European Romani women arrive in this country today still following the practice they are accused of child-cruelty! So much for tolerance or accepting differing cultures.)

Eli, it transpired, was working in partnership with one of his cousins, who resided with his elderly parents in a small timber-framed bungalow between Weymouth and Bridport. The old father, however, had become a trifle dissatisfied with his modest dwelling and was about to have it replaced by a new home, to be delivered in sections and erected within a few hours.

His son, Albert was thrilled at the prospect, quite boastful in fact.

"They'm reliverin' un next week," he told me. "Tis one o' they sexual bungalows – they can put un up in an hour!"

Although I knew such a feat of constructions was impossible, even by the keenest hands, I did not question the truth of his statement. Albert, then in his forties, had remained at home with his parents whilst his siblings, two girls, had flown the nest long before both marrying Travellers.

"Be nice for me dear old Mam," he observed. "And for me dear old Dad, too I suppose. Once he's in there I bet he'll cock his legs up for the rest of his life. Dear ole *mush* – comin' eighty year old this Christmas, an' still smokin' like a fuckin' chimbley!"

Albert had arrived on a bicycle, having never mastered the art of driving,

When his father, in a fit of misplaced hope, had purchased him a superior old Lancashire car, cut-down with a truck body, of 1939 vintage, his nerve had failed. Even the fact of the vehicle having the undoubted advantage of 'pre-selected' gears, and the mysteries of a 'fluid-flywheel,' it was rejected as un-driveable by the pernickety Albert – to the utter disgust of Young Jobi.

Hence Eli, another non-driver, and Albert, in their business as 'tree-loppers' maintained an admirable simplicity of equipment for their enterprise. One bow-saw, two lengths of rope, and a pair of shears, plus their two bicycles, were their complement.

Once Eli and Albert had ridden off on their bicycles, each with a length of rope professionally encircling their shoulders, the bow-saw and shears tied to the handlebars of each other's cycle, we were left along except for the huddle of small to middle-sized children left behind. They could be trusted not to leave the fireside, nor converse with any strangers who might happen by. It all seemed a sensible arrangement to me.

We decided to have an uncharacteristically lazy and relaxed day: a penny unspent was a penny saved.

We both realised that it was but a temporary lapse from the incessant toil that our new life-style would demand: even to keep financially afloat would be an achievement in itself. In that ambition one was not alone; the numbers of Travellers following the same path, with astonishingly different results, was evident to those with the ability to perceive it. Everything was on view.

In those times, before the construction of Council Sites, with their aim of hiding Travellers away in desolate industrial areas, or behind high walls, or sometimes both, they gradually became the only recourse for those Travellers unwilling, or unable, to bear the constant harrying and persecution heaped upon them. These were a people for whom the feeling of freedom, the ability to wander from one temporary stopping-place to another was removed by governmental decree. To be thus enclosed was anathema to them, especially in the joyless fenced-off plots provided: tarmac and concrete-filled, with no flowers or any form of vegetation, sterility was surely the aim.

After such a day of rest we went to bed early, our intent to leave the next morning. Indeed, with the remnants of a mist, the sun breaking through, we were up and ready just as the others were emerging from their night's rest.

After brief farewells, and my promise to Young Jobi that I would contact him soon, hopefully with the documentation that would change his life, we were ready to go.

With no hesitation the engine of the Bedford fired and, with the expulsion of a little blue smoke and some heartening revs, we were off and away. We had decided on taking the route via Dorchester, Blandford and Shaftesbury. Once leaving the latter we would enter a new world. I felt the desire to spend no time dawdling in the town of Dorchester, but perhaps to have a break for some victuals when we were within the little town of Blandford Forum.

When we were not far from Dorchester we passed the vast manorial residence of a retired sheep-farmer whose fortune was apparently accrued in the countries of both New Zealand and Australia, so local legend proclaimed. This amiable millionaire of such financial capability remained in my memory rather more because of his exotic wife than himself. The latter, whom I met on only one occasion under unlikely circumstances, was the daughter of Diego Rivera the Mexican artist of great repute. His daughter Marika was one the more surprising aspects of the millionaire sheep-farmer's life. To the casual onlooker their union was something of a mystery. Dark-suited and executive of appearance, his persona seemed in direct contrast to the Latin ebullience which surrounded his wife. Her curiosity value was further enhanced by her ever-present ninety years old Russian mother: a silent and closed-in figure, simmering quietly in her shadow. Marika, like most flamboyant eccentrics, was a pleasure to look upon. I would like to have known her.

(Oddly enough, some forty years later, I happened to be strolling down the High Street in Oxford when I noticed a poster advertising 'An Evening with Marika Rivera' at a local church hall. It purported to contain both her acclaimed Mexican dancing, and also tales of her pre-war years in Paris in the company of Picasso, and various luminaries of the art world of that era. Unhappily a variety of circumstances prevented my attending the one-night event, (a missed opportunity that I greatly regret).

From Dorchester, not far from the agreeably-named village of Piddlehinton, we passed by a small empty field, its nearest habitation a smartened-up thatched cottage.

I was saddened to perceive the little paddock empty, for, years before, it had housed the residential bus-conversion home of an elderly retired show woman who settled there after giving up her itinerant life of travelling with the fairs, offering toffee-apples and ping-pong ball sized sweets of a flavour so powerful that all but the most hardened of palates found them inedible. However, showmanship won, and her sales of the invidious confectionary never seemed to flag. She was known, by both fans and foes, as 'The Gobstopper Queen.' Yet one more, if tiny, light had gone out.

It was mid-morning as we reached Blandford. By chance it was market day so we decided to inspect its offerings, after having the luck of finding a parking-space within easy distance of the stalls. My eye was instantly caught by a rug and carpet seller. It was the person of old Boucher Black, a Traveller long-since absent from the itinerant life: he was living in a new bungalow of uncommon splendour near to Southampton.

Toffee apples

Then in his late sixties he had begun the gradual slowing-down process of old age: like all of his years, after lives spent in the uphill battle for survival assisted by the consumption of alcohol imbibed with reckless disregard to health, he had reached the pitch when Time Was His Enemy.

Seated at the back of his stall, wearing a well-tailored striped suit, white-collared shirt and foulard silk tie, he gave every impression of being the successful business man – which of course he was.

Drawn up nearby was a new 30cwt Bedford A-type van, painted in a refined two-toned grey. It was a vehicle much favoured by carpet-hawkers. The two rear doors were propped open to display samples of his more inspiring stock, the form of remarkably subdued designs and colouration having been the aim of the makers. Boucher had placed a discreet notice beside them announcing their origins to be both Turkey and Persia. None but the most courageous would attempt an argument on that score.

Boucher, whom I had known for some ten years, was one of those people, not to be despised, for whom success on his own terms was not enough. Lest it should go unnoticed he would invariably follow the course of ramming it home in search of admiration, sometimes inadvertently misjudging the person to whom he was boasting, with dangerous results. I once saw him floored in a public house by a man for whom he was buying a drink: his mistake was, before offering payment over the bar, to draw a thick wad of twenty-pound notes, from his trouser pocket, peeling one off with a wink.

"You don't have to show us your fucking *loover* (money) Boucher. You braggy bastard – have that!" sneered the man.

It was a mighty blow, witnessed by most with some approval, rendering Boucher to near unconsciousness and unable to retaliate. Not, of course, that he had learned from it, and continued on his chosen path. Personally, I was never offended nor felt slighted by such conduct, accepting it as a facet of his character to be viewed with nonchalance.

"How are you, Boucher?" I enquired.

"Poor but happy," he smiled, his small eyes narrowing to slits, whilst his longish snow-white hair played tag with the gusts of wind which swirled it into tufts.

"Where you out at?" he asked, knowing I was not settled-down.

I apprised him of our situation and I could see he viewed it with some contempt.

"You wants to get yourself a bit of a place somewhere," he advised. "The old Travellers' life is finished, *mush*, an' the Irish is gonna fuck-up what's left of it, you'll see," he added.

In some ways his opinion was justified – in another totally inaccurate. It was before the advent of the elegant trailers manufactured for an ever-growing number of Travellers who, as in Waggon-Time, desired that the trailers should become more and more elegant, ornate, rococo, even vulgar: opulence was the goal. In the following two decades such aims were achieved by several firms – at the peak of the producers were the 'Vickers' of Morecambe and the 'Westmorland Star' of Penrith. Eventually both of these were discontinued owing to the increasing costs of all that was entailed in their construction. One or two other makers have followed in their wake, but without exciting results. Alas, most Travellers have been seduced by German trailers – soulless, fragile, and lacking the 'homeliness' of their British forbears, they bring little satisfaction apart from their lightness (a Transit van would not shy at their aplitude).

"See my place?" he began. "I just been offered a hundred grand for it."

"Going to sell it?" I asked, already knowing the answer.

"Nar!" he remonstrated. "I could do with the money, mind. I'm a proper old needy, *mush* – you knows that."

He ran a diamond-ringed finger through his hair, grinning cynically at me.

"I wish I had your money, Boucher," I answered, saying what I knew he would like to hear. "What's it like being a millionaire?"

"Millionaire! I wishes I was – the fuckin' tax man keeps on trying get some of it. I tried to keep him sweet with a nice pair of *chordi choks* (stolen boots) but he wouldn't have none of it."

At such injustice we momentarily looked glum. A mood which was not alleviated when I asked after his health.

"Oh, my mate," he cried. "I got this poxy regina – looked like *mullerin'* (killing) me. Anyway I bin up to London an' seen this private specialist doctor man. He's gid me some tablets what he swears'll get me right. An' I should fuckin' think so at fifty pounds for each one!"

"Lucky you've got the money to pay for 'em," I observed.

"Hm!" he grunted. "Another fifty of 'em an' I'll be down the Poor House!"

We smiled at this, and after a few more minutes, seeing Beshlie approaching, we parted, him insisting on giving me his telephone number – a fortunate occurrence it later transpired.

Beshlie had obtained some food, for both ourselves and the livestock, from the market-place. Hence our departure was not delayed and we soon found ourselves on the main road which would pass through Iwerne Minster, then Fontwell Magna and on to Shaftesbury. I planned to spend a night on what was known to the Travellers as 'Shaftesbury Common' before heading on towards Frome the next day. After negotiating a few hills, both up and down, we arrived at our destination.

To our slight surprise there were already people there. A little distance from us was a little, shabby, egg-shaped trailer of hardboard, made before the advent of aluminium; one window in the side was cracked, and the door was ill-fitting. Parked a few yards away there was a small pre-war Ford van, hand-painted in dark maroon. A fragile-looking vee-shaped tow-bar projected from the rear: both time and drivers had left their mark upon it. The greatest amongst the brotherhood of motor-salesmen would have found it difficult to promote this van – to even the most down-trodden potential customer.

The remains of a *yog* still smouldered beside the little home; a thick iron 'crane' supported a large black kettle. As we stopped an uncivil-looking lurcher emerged from one end of the trailer's chassis and a rough-coated terrier from the other. Both emitted hostile barks and strained at their chains, each attached to the trailer. Outraged by the noises from invisible foes Naylor replied with growls and subdued barks.

Upon such commotion the trailer door was opened and out stepped a young man, in his mid-twenties. He was wearing a broad-brimmed felt hat and a cross-tied silk scarf of cheery pattern in yellow and red: his features were of a cast that I had seen in Hampshire.

He was followed by his wife and little daughter. Both were fair-haired and blue-eyed but still of very Romani features. Both mother and daughter had their hair in braids, clipped back from their foreheads by matching blue slides: each had dark hazel eyes. They were, without doubt, an attractive and pleasingly old-fashioned looking little family.

It did not take long to establish communication. The man, whose first name was Winky, was still part of Hampshire in his own mind. With many relatives still travelling and others settled-down there. A few, in fact, resident in one of the notorious New Forest Compounds. His wife, though, was a Buckland, with most of her relatives in the county of Oxfordshire. With such information I was able to astonish them with my knowledge of her family-tree: a knack which has held me in good stead on countless occasions.

The woman was named Rosina and the child Little Rosina. I was glad to let her know that I was well-acquainted with her uncle, who was known as 'Side-neck Jim.' This appellation was given after he had been badly injured as a child in an accident, and had emerged from hospital with his head and neck permanently to one side on his shoulders. Luckily it did not seem to stunt his chances in life, even giving him a certain degree of fame.

They had themselves not been motorised for long, they told me, and were pondering seriously on returning to horses. I could not help, privately, but feel it might be their wisest course. A few hours of desultory conversation with the undeniably pleasant Winky, however, had seemed to characterise the men who had successfully made the leap.

(Some years later we were stopping on a roadside at a place with the evocative name of Goosey Green in Berkshire when I was accosted by a local resident who had come to investigate us. He airily announced to me: "We used to get a lot of gypsies round here, with horses and painted caravans – nice people, we never had any trouble with them." Pointing to some black rings where fires had been not long since, I said: "Well, I can see the fire places – someone must have stopped here."

"Oh yes – bloody London scrap-dealers with old lorries and caravans. They are a damned nuisance, leaving filth and rubbish everywhere. Whenever I see them here I call the police – they soon deal with them!"

His smugness and self-righteousness was utterly depressing. London scrap-dealers indeed! The people whom he had just denounced were, in fact, direct descendants of the 'nice people' whose qualities had remained in his memory. To try to disabuse him would inevitably lead to no kind of victory. Prejudice can rarely be dislodged).

Despite their faltering resolution permanently to adopt motorisation, Winky was able to boast that his little Ford van had hauled them up a notoriously steep hill, encountered on the road to the finely-named Tollard Royal, with its gradients of 1 in 4 and its numerous hair-pin bends, we had once thrown caution to the winds and rashly descended it with horse and waggon. Going downwards was harrowing enough. To ascend it was unthinkable. Not without reason was it named Zig-Zag Hill, a name worthily amended by Winky to "Shig-Shag Hill!"

Looking at the subdued little van I was hard put to accept the truth of his assertion: it was a doubt that I kept to myself.

Parking the Bedford in the lee of some bushes we set ourselves up for the night, intent of leaving in the morning. Like most habitually-used Travellers' *atchin' tans* (stopping places) there was a scarcity of wood for the fire. Indeed even the most ardent scavenging produced barely sufficient for our cooking-fire, and just a few twigs for the morning.

"Nairn a bit of *kosh* (wood) anywhere, *mush*," said Winky mournfully, adding, "Old Monty an' his lot've bin here for a week – burnt every bit there was. We bin havin' to fetch some back wi' us when we goes out. An' as for a drop of *pani* (water) the old *mush* at the garage charges five shillings to fill up a milk churn even though we gits the petrol there."

There is no doubt that meanness of spirit is not as rare as one could wish.

We departed from the common by nine o'clock in the morning, by which hour Winky and his wife and daughter were sitting round their fire, a hoop-handled frying pan filled with lumps of bacon sizzling enticingly. By the time of our leaving we said our farewells and the three of them stood waving forlornly as we bumped across the rutted grassland and on to the road.

To those with the innate sophistication of today our first little motoring safari might appear to be one of no temerity, hardly worth a mention. Yet for us, on the very edge of new beginnings, it all became filled with significance; so many tests lay ahead.

From Shaftesbury we headed out on the main road, eventually branching off to Mere, and then Maiden Bradley, going on towards Frome. Hardly had we passed through Maiden Bradley, when our dreads became a reality in the shape of ominous creakings and thuddings issuing from, as far as we could judge, somewhere in the region of the rear axle. As I had never even replaced a sparking plug, let alone having allowed myself the pleasure of changing a wheel, the uneasy sounds, seeming to increase in ferocity, did little to assuage our fears. Thus, unaware of what fate had in store for us, we continued at an ever-slowing pace, my optimism fading fast.

Rounding a bend we were delighted to see a Travellers bungalow, adjoined by a scrap yard, and beside that there was a field of half an acre or more, in which were dotted a variety of lorries and vans. Some gave the appearance of being complete, others had been partially dismembered for the provision of spare parts.

A man emerged from the bungalow and we drew to a halt. He was a Traveller, of the sort who cultivated a respectable, even neat, appearance, hoping that it would benefit him in his business enterprises. Dark complexioned, black-haired, with strong features, he was well-served by his blue-serge suit and white shirt. Only the presence of a heavy 'plaited' gold-ring on the third finger of his left hand might have hinted at his Traveller connections.

We introduced ourselves, and he to us as Morris Black. After a few minutes of conversation in which we explained our hazardous position he became very helpful, coming up with a variety of suggestions. Just then a dark blue 30cwt Bull nose Bedford lorry drove into the scrap yard.

"Here's Albi," said Morris. "He's better with motors that I am."

Albi, unlike Morris, seemed to flaunt his Romani appearance. Dressed in a snap-brim felt hat, coloured neckerchief, and Traveller-style suit tailored to the fashion of the moment, with yoke back, turn-back cuffs, and a number of extra pockets with button-down flaps, he was a figure to be admired.

I told him of our troubles and he reacted with commendable assurance.

"You got the half-shaft gone in the back axle – you won't get far like that."

Both Beshlie and I felt depressed.

"The best thing to do is to pull in that field an' to put in a different back axle. You got one, ain't you, Morris?"

"Dunno," said Morris.

"Course you have," replied Albi confidently. "We could take the one off Black Bill's old lorry – he's over in the corner. Someone's bought the engine, but they ain't touched the axles."

Thus without more ado we drove in across the field, to park near to the lorry once belonging to Black Bill. Albi, who seemed slightly fascinated by us, agreed to assist in the task in the company of Morris and his eldest son, a pleasant youth named Sam.

It was agreed with Morris that we could light a small fire to cook our evening meal, using whatever we wanted from a pile of old decking and boards which lay in a heap a few yards from where we had parked.

In one way I was overtaken by relief in the way that fortune would yet again smile upon us, though I was not unaware of the risks implied.

We cooked our meal in subdued spirits, neither Beshlie's pessimism nor my optimism seemed capable of penetrating the black cloud which hung over us. To be in a situation of complete ignorance, entirely in the hands of others, no matter how good-hearted they might be, was one with which I was unfamiliar. Hence it was a case of needs must: Morris and Albi were our eyes and our guides.

The next morning dawned dank and wet, a thin drizzle permeating the surrounding landscape. We enjoyed a hasty breakfast of oatmeal porridge and black tea, and managed to finish it before the stocky figures of Morris and Albi came striding towards us, clad in workmanlike boiler suits, though without the abandonment of Albi's snap-brim trilby.

They entered into cautious inspection both of the desolate lorry of Black Bill, and then our own. Luckily it was found that both vehicles were close in age, both the same model, so in that respect the complications were but few.

"I only hope the h'axle's all right on Bill's old motor," said Morris mournfully.

"He's all right – Bill druv him in here," announced Albi cheerfully. When he fetched him in here all he needed was a new engine – the old one blowed-up outside the gate wi' no warning at all. Fuckin' hell, you should a-seen Bill's face!"

"Well, what do you think? Want to take a chance, kid?" Morris enquired.

There appeared to be little alternative: it was a gamble I would take. Beshlie's face remained impassive, but I could sense her dubiosity.

The two commenced work with enthusiasm, collecting planks, jacks, and other tools from a dark-looking shed nearby, assisted to some degree by the youth Sam. Our little home was elevated with precision, and within a surprisingly short time our red-wheeled back axle was removed, lying on the oily grass.

The same procedure was effectively copied on the lorry. All that was left was hope. In times like that one regretted the absence of any orthodox religious beliefs upon which we could call for spiritual sustenance. Alas, however, mythology has never figured largely in my life, apart from a youthful delight in the magnificent *Grimm's Fairy Tales*. However, not having a volume to hand I was unable to reap any benefits from its consumption, whilst the transplant operation proceeded to plan.

Taking a short respite from their intensive labour, Morris and Albi each rolled a cigarette and inhaled deeply: the comforting odour of their Black Beauty tobacco hanging delicately in the damp air.

For me tension was mounting as the operation proceeded. At that point I decided that, whatever the outcome of the axle exchange, the days of the Bedford, our first motor, were limited: it had not shown itself to be in possession of the most vital attribute demanded of it: namely, it had not proved to be a 'lucky motor.' By such seemingly-innocuous behaviour can humans, animals, and machines be accurately judged by the discerning.

As an instance of such unluckiness, I can cite a brand-new, canary yellow, pick-up truck that I once bought in 1970. We were stopping at Cambridge, and on the *first day,* just after I had collected it from the sales showroom, I was pulled up, for no good reason, by the police, which was inconvenient.

On the *second*, whilst out calling, I was signalled to halt by a passing Police 'jam-sandwich' patrol car: indignation and shock were my interpolation, being met with a cold response.

The very next day I drove to a Bedford agent in a neighbouring town and, with the offer of instant cash in the transaction, was able to negotiate an exchange deal of a not *entirely* unsatisfactory nature. The vehicle involved in the exchange was a van – a model hailed as a rival to the Ford. However, without the comforts or certain refinements of the latter its success was rather limited. For Travellers its main advantage lay in the fact of its being very low-geared, and thus able to pull trailers of exacting weight up even the steepest of gradients with impunity. In that ability it achieved respect. Sadly, as the legendary name of Bedford eventually disappeared and production ceased, so it vanished forever.

To us, untutored spectators that we were, the sight of the men performing their task with calm determination filled us with admiration and respect. A respect by no means diminished when, after six or seven hours, the labour was deemed a success. A trial run at a cautious pace around the field proved surprisingly beneficial to our spirits. The moment of reckoning was at hand. Albi and Morris each lit a cigarette and stood smiling sheepishly – trusting, like us, that their handiwork would be a success. Indeed the sum asked by Morris seemed entirely reasonable and I removed it secretively from a wad of notes – our worldly capital – and paid them.

Albi was, apparently, something of a legend throughout Somerset in regards to his mechanical capabilities with Bedfords. We only hoped that his talents were not on the wane!

Marooned in strange country, as we had been, we consulted together and decided to return to Fryern to lick our wounds and decide on our future. We were both deeply aware of our good fortune in being able to enjoy such a haven.

Hence with feelings of nervous strain and unwanted tension we bid Morris and Albi farewell and set off. I felt inclined to take the road to Salisbury, passing through Wyle. Once at Salisbury it was but a fairly short journey to Fryern; about a dozen miles I thought.

To my private astonishment the van's acceptance of the transplant appeared to cause no mechanical malfunction. In fact, our progress seemed smoother than on our outward journey. As ever financially straitened circumstance hung heavily over our heads. Not for us the ease of Social Security: our only recourse was our own ingenuity and an innate desire to 'struggle for a shilling,' in the spirit of the traditional dealing-men of that era.

It was early afternoon when we slid back into the field at Fryern, ending –up beside the waggon.

The faintest touch of autumn was in the air and we felt that, with the added comfort of a Queenie Stove, the waggon would be our first choice of accommodation.

Chapter 4

Another Maiden Voyage

This was a period in our lives when events moved speedily, by unexpected turns of fate, and we found ourselves in possession of a new (to us) trailer and an ex U.S. Army long-wheel-based Jeep.

The trailer caravan, some 12ft in length, was completely devoid of either style or charm; its only attraction lay in its value as a stepping-stone in a new mode of existence. It was of some age and of slightly warped appearance, so aged in fact that it was constructed of hardboard and not of aluminium, universally adopted later. True to another fashion of its period it was painted in a gloomy shade of dark green and a deep cream, which later manufacturers have had wisdom enough to abandon in favour of lighter and more imaginative colour combinations. I had noticed it standing in a garden, sporting a roughly painted 'For Sale' notice.

The owner proved to be a large, fat, sagging man of early middle-age, with greasy fair hair, long and thin on top and scraped off abruptly around the back and sides: an unattractive though oddly common style of coiffure. His face was flabby, flecked with uneven stubble, unhealthily smooth, and his mouth was very small like a tea-pot spout. In his eyes their shone a light of avarice and greed which made me feel faintly sympathetic towards him.

"What do you want for the old trailer?" I asked, nothing if not direct.

"You interested in 'im?" he returned.

"Might be – depends on the price," I replied, eyeing him narrowly.

"I'll take seventy-five pounds for 'im, mate," he said airily, offering me a Woodbine cigarette.

"Will you?" I answered nonchalantly. "Well, let's have a look inside before we talk about that."

He went into the cottage, came back with the key and we stepped inside the trailer. It smelt both musty and damp and was remarkably shabby. An old mat lay on the floor, over cracked linoleum, and the only decoration was an out-of-date calendar hanging on the wall. The latter had obviously been provided by a benevolent business firm, whose product was boldly inscribed around the edges, whilst the pictorial attraction was an expansively mammiferous young lady with an engaging smile.

Our eyes had simultaneously rested upon the mural decoration for an instant, and our glances met.

"I wishes it was bloody spring, mate," remarked the man, the ghost of a smile flickering across his pudgy features.

I proceeded to inspect the exterior and the interior of the caravan, drawing in my breath slowly in affected horror at various small faults I discovered, and prodding wordlessly at odd cracks and damaged parts to let the man see that they had not escaped my notice. Finally, having examined it fully, and commented on the poor state of the trailer caravan market in general at that time, I offered him twenty-five pounds for it as a test offer. Had he been a more contemptible sort of man he would probably have been genuinely insulted and might well have refused to continue any transaction. As it was, however, he gave what for him passed as a smile and rejected the offer.

"I don't blame you for trying," he said, "but I shouldn't take no less than sixty-five pounds cash for 'im – he's worth more'n twenty-five for a store shed."

"You know what they say – one bidder's worth a hundred lookers-on!" I re-joined, reminding him of the old dealer's adage.

"I knows all about that – an' I agrees with you," he responded. "But I ain't gonna give the bloody thing away, mate."

After a small amount of further haggling we eventually met at fifty pounds, which I rather grudgingly paid him in cash, agreeing to have the trailer moved within as short a time as possible.

At this point the vagaries of fate took hold of events. It was mid-morning when a small ex-M.O.D. van drew up short at the gate, emitting rather uneven blasts on the horn, hoping to engage our attention. I walked over to the gate, to be greeted by a gaunt-faced man, his face the colour of pickled-cabbage, wearing a 'pork-pie' hat of a blackish hue and a Traveller-style many-pocketed, yoke-backed, suit.

"Hullo, my old cousin," he remarked. "How's your luck?"

"Not so good as yours," I replied, smiling slightly.

"I'm fucked-up an' far from home – can't earn a shilling!"

We both grinned, digesting the unlikelihood of his statement being true.

"Do you want to sell the Bedford van?" he enquired, perceiving it across the field.

"I *would* sell it or I'd *chop* (exchange) it for a little lorry," I replied, with a certain greenness.

"I tell you what I *have* got," said he, leaping at the opportunity. "I got a nice little long-wheel-base Jeep, with a wood drop-side body. Ain't done no miles – runs like new – I kin fetch her over if you think we might have a deal. I'd have to be in the drawing-room, mind, an' have a bit of *loover* (money) to *chop*."

"Other way round, I'd say – mine's a lovely clean old Bedford."

"Oh *dordi*! There's a man! But I'll try to have deal with you. How about if I drives the little motor over tomorrow an' you can have a look. I reckons it's just the motor for you – she'd tow a trailer easy. An' with the bit of four-wheel drive you wouldn't get stuck in no mud."

In the blissful ignorance of my first motoring days I was willing to chance anything, beside which I had always fancied the exciting all-terrain accomplishments of such sturdy vehicles.

Hence it was arranged that he would bring the Jeep over from his 'yard' near Southampton. He inspected the Bedford and, apart from its undeniable mileage, it appeared to meet with his guarded approval.

We spent the rest of the day removing the appendages we had added in order for it to be a 'motor-home' whilst we were living in it. Already we had established the trailer in the field, and were now engaged in its transformation both inside and out.

A brief visit to the home of Gilly Gayle provided us with enough half-full tins of paint, in a variety of colours, to complete the re-decoration of the trailer to an approximation of our aim. Black, yellow, and red were the colourations applied to the exterior which proved to be, if not endearing, at least dramatic, perhaps even leaning faintly backwards in the shadow of waggon-times.

Beshlie, whose innate ability to improvise even the most unpromising of material into something approaching beauty, spent a few days labouring towards that goal. The result, something between an Aladdin's Cave and a Victorian boudoir, met all our requirements.

The Southampton-based Traveller, named Isaac, arrived the following day: the Jeep's engine whirring smoothly.

He emerged, this time his purple features accentuated by the presence of a bright check hat: a slightly uneasy union.

We stood gazing at the Jeep: it was painted in a discreet shade of battleship grey and appeared to be devoid of dents or scrapes. The wooden body, obviously the work of some jobbing-carpenter, sat firmly aboard the rear.

"One owner after the Yanks," Isaac proudly informed me, adding, "an' only 22,000 miles on the clock – ain't hardly run-in."

There was about this mildly eccentric vehicle a quality that appealed to me. It was, of course, long before I realised that being in 'original' condition was key in its valuation. The more 'personalised' it had been by a previous loving owner the less its commercial value became. A sad fact of life to learn by experience.

In any event, with Beshlie's cautious approval, I commenced a long battle of wills with the rather intransigent Isaac.

"That motor stand me in at more'n that, my old cousin," he asserted when I valued it at seventy pounds and asked him for thirty to *chop*.

It took several cups of tea, and over an hour before we eventually reached an understanding – not one greatly advantageous to me, but possibly more so than I had anticipated.

In a moment of what I would probably regard as lunacy today, I gave him but seven pounds to effect the exchange. Happily it was not a decision that I was later to regret.

At least there were two months' tax remaining on the licence disc.

The acquisition of a left-hand drive motor, to one so new to driving, did not bring about the neuroses and uncertainties that must surely have prevailed in anyone used to many years of right-hand driving only.

Indeed, so unhinged with excitement were we by our new turnout that I decided, for our maiden-voyage of trailer-towing, to make for Blandford in Dorset, in the locality of which town were several much-frequented Travellers' stopping-places whereon one could always snatch a few days before being moved-on. There came to mind at once: 'Lady Float Over the Trees,' 'Dinile's Corner' and 'Sows Leap.'

I chose the first, which was a wide drove, up a hill, not far from the village of Stourpaine. We had enough money to last for two or three weeks – giving us some time to adjust to our new form of living. However, I thought that we might just spend a week or so away from Fryern, returning there hopefully to sell the waggon and to allow the portrait of Beshlie to proceed. We were deeply aware of that opportunity being there as a choice for us. We had not experienced such a luxury before.

Fortunately the U.S. Jeep had a tow-bar already affixed, with a ball-hitch tee – though without the benefit of an 'electrics' plug. The absence of the latter prevented the association of rear lights, brake lights or signal indicators. In those days the absence of the latter appendages was not viewed with the horror, or prosecution, that would be evoked today.

I found my first-time towing of a trailer-caravan peculiarly satisfying, though fraught with a tension factor only exceeded, one surmises, by those intrepid enough to devote themselves to the exploration of outer space! The Jeep, despite only being equipped with a three-speed gearbox, manfully propelled our little home, engine running smoothly, and the 'balloon' tyres producing a characteristic high-pitched whining sound on the tarmac road.

It was about two hours after leaving Fryern that we ascended the hill, previously only undertaken with horse and waggon, and soon espied the opening of the drove known as 'Lady Float Over the Trees' by generations of old-fashioned Travellers. Doubtless the reason for its evocative title lay buried far back in time.

In yet another new achievement for me I reversed the trailer into the entrance of the drove, not too far, though, as I wished to avoid the possibility of our exit being blocked by an inconsiderate arrival – an occurrence, alas, far from uncommon.

On both sides of the drove were black rings, the fire-places of Travellers not long gone. Scraps of coloured wools caught in the hawthorne hedge, a few old tins and a discarded mattress assisted in the provision of a homely atmosphere. All, except the few tins, would be devoured by the forces of nature in a surprisingly short time, I knew.

Further still up the drove were several grazed-down circular rings where horses had been tethered on their 'plug' chains. In many ways it was a nostalgic scene for us.

In those innocent fargone days Travellers, in 'their own country' would frequently leave their belongings unattended during the day whilst they were out 'calling,' with no fear that anything might be stolen. Alas, however, no such carefree circumstances exist today – Travellers have even, in rare incidents, fallen into such a moral abyss that they have carried out robberies on their fellows, even though they are often living in conditions of wealth undreamed-of by their less-demanding forbears.

Hence, the next morning we decided to drive into Blandford, both to look around and to buy some food.

The Jeep started rather hesitantly but fired after the third try: not a good omen.

As we descended the hill towards Stourpaine we saw two somewhat colour-less and broken-down-looking waggons, both of the square-bowed 'Dorset' open-lot construction, on a wide verge beside the main road. Without either trees or bushes nearby they were afforded little protection or privacy.

As we came closer I could see several adults and two or three half-grown children crouched around a stick fire. I recognised them at once: There was Bob'n'Alli and some of their younger children and two rough-looking middle-aged men, brothers who had remained single and were called Jobi and Toby. They had both lived with their mother until she died, their numerous brothers and sisters having all flown the nest decades before. I had met their ancient mother, called Dosha, once only.

She had remained indelibly lodged in my memory after her informing me, whilst discussing her family, that owing to their large number she had been driven to calling her youngest son Jobi, despite it being the name of her first-born.

"I had to call un Jobi," she explained. "Cos we had so many boys we runned out've names!"

Against such reasoning there was no polite argument.

There was about the little gathering an air of some desolation; almost, in a sense, a resignation that they were indeed clinging to what had almost become the fag-end, as it were, of a disappearing way of life.

The two brothers, their features heavily lined and impassive, nodded a greeting, simultaneously rolling themselves a thin Black Beauty cigarette. I knew them of old, and appreciated their singular lack of addiction to any form of conversation.

"They'm two brothers like deaf newts – you c'ain't git no sensible talk out've either one on 'em," their mother had remarked to me in some disgust.

Bob'n'Alli, or Bob and Alice to give them their full names, remained stoically by the *yog* (fire), Alli frying some thin strips of fatty bacon in a hoop-handled pan, black and well-used.

Three children, two boys and one very dishevelled-looking girl, sat expectantly awaiting the strip of bacon wrapped in a piece of white bread that would soon come their way.

Two cross-bred rough-coated lurchers the size of Bedlingtons, lay as near to the fire as they dared, anxious for the scraps which would be cast in their direction.

They growled a little at my approach.

"Goo an' lay down, dogs!" Bob shouted at them, and they slunk a little further from the fire.

After a short conversation, and a mug of sweet but milk-less tea, we had discussed all that was relevant to our lives and were perilously near to 'running out of talk' – fortunately not a common occurrence.

"I ain't never seed no Jeep made into a newtility," observed Bob, pointing at the bodywork's transformation into a lorry.

Taking our leave it was not long before we were in Blandford, a little town quite well-known to us.

We had just completed our food purchases and were on our way back to the Jeep when we were accosted in the street by a young woman of eighteen or twenty years of age.

After the publication of my first book *Smoke In The Lane'* in 1958 it was not entirely unknown for us to be approached by strangers: it was our first experience of Minor Celebrity Status. An experience that I have taken every known precaution to avoid during the succeeding fifty plus years!

However, in this instance our attention was firmly gripped by the unnerving stature, long blonde hair, and features of an arresting beauty.

There was about this young woman the kind of confidence that radiates from those fortunately-born persons for whom life should hold no problems other than those of their own making. Education from expensive tutoring, unlimited wealth, success in a chosen field, and a Scandinavian beauty in a willowy frame. All that I could see at a glance – but little did I realise that she was a member of one of England's richest and most privileged families. It was all a long way from our world.

This encounter took place in pre-hippy days, indeed during that short-lived period of time when it was 'beatniks' who ruffled social feathers. Possibly the most socially elevated persons who fell, if only temporarily, under its spell were the Lords Valentine and Christopher Thynne of Longleat, Jeremy Sandford the writer, and numerous would-be eccentrics and socialites known jokily as 'Hooray Henrys.'

The garb of this young woman reflected the fashion affected by this quasi sect; namely sheepskin coat, short skirt and black woollen stockings. For males the wearing of narrow denim jeans and suede jacket was essential. Whilst the addition of cowboy boots and black or tartan shirts were viewed with favour. Sideburns and slightly longer hair than hitherto sported were yet another fashion affected by the so-called 'beatniks,' especially those from wealthy backgrounds. All, one gathered, influenced by the writer Jack Keruac, whose written word and reported life-style amalgamated to confer upon him almost mythic status: a strange and inexplicable happening of the period, to last so short a time and to seem so peculiar in retrospect. It was my only brush with the upper reaches of Society; indeed since then they appear to have avoided me.

From the conversation of the young woman, rejoicing in the faintly exotic name of Suna, we learned that she was having a waggon built for her by a local carpenter whose knowledge of waggons was not extensive. Therefore, she suggested, a visit from us to his workshop to scan his progress would be regarded with gratitude. It was a request, if only for its novelty value, that we felt unable to turn down.

Thus it was arranged that we would be transported there in the family car, and a time was agreed upon. At the appointed hour, the next day, our attention was diverted by the sudden presence of an elegant apple-green Bentley limousine, chauffeur-driven, inside which the figure of Suna could be detected, resting comfortably on one of the ivory-coloured leather cushions benevolently provided as head-rests. As the owners of an ex-US Jeep and an aged trailer caravan we were naturally subdued by such tasteful ostentation.

Entering the luxurious conveyance, and feeling it gliding noiselessly down the hill, was to experience a different world: was it one to be viewed as an aspiration, a wistful ambition? Who could say?

Later in life, from the nineteen seventies onwards, I have seen a number of Travellers rising to such financial heights that they have afforded such opulence. And, with but few exceptions they have, to my mind, richly deserved such regards in payment for their toil and wizardry.

Upon entering the workshop we perceived that the waggon was but a work in progress, as it were. The carpenter, a leather-aproned and somewhat morose-looking man of middle age, showed little friendliness towards us, or indeed, to the instigator of his efforts. As the rear wheels were large and running outside the beginnings of the body, I presumed that he had a Reading waggon in mind as a model. However, questioning on my part provoked little but grunts and his gaze grew even more distant.

Hence, without any discernible advantages, we departed the workshop slightly gloomily. However, we were invited to afternoon tea by Suna, which we accepted mainly out of curiosity.

The drive from the waggon-builder to the spacious home, set in its own grounds, with the added charm of being out of both sight and sound of any form of neighbours. It was the archetypal model of a middle-sized country estate.

On entering the house, through a spacious porch and an impressively panelled front door, we were met by Suna's mother, a rather forbidding square-faced woman with an air of authority, her fair-coloured hair strictly coiffed into the style which was to be immortalised by Mrs Thatcher during her time as Prime Minister. Each hair was moulded into exact union with its fellows, resistance was subjugated at once.

We sat down by a low table and were offered cups of aromatic tea, and a choice of delicately shaped biscuits which were unfamiliar to me.

It could hardly be judged a successful occasion, bedevilled by ceaseless questions, arched eyebrows, and non-committal replies.

Fortunately, perhaps, we were interrupted by the arrival of a taxi from which a handsome, but tottering, figure of a youth was escorted by the driver.

"Oh God! It's Mikey," exclaimed Suna, "and he's a drunk!"

The matriarch hastened from the table and assisted the taxi driver in supporting his ashen-faced, unsteady, passenger upstairs to his room.

So distraught were both Suna and her mother by the sudden and unexpected intrusion that years of inherited social mores fled by the board; we were left abandoned, tea-cups and biscuits our only company. However, after a few minutes we were joined by the Hon. Owner of the house, who presented himself and cleverly disguised what must have been astonishment at our appearance. Although only of early middle-age there was about his person signs of a life lived without any sacrifice of the surfeits and satiety so easily accessible to one in his position. With thinning black hair, and encroaching flabbiness in both face and form, he was obviously a person in deterioration of his own doing.

His manner, however, was both genial and polite – and the appearance of his dissolute offspring apparently caused him less discomfort than it had to his wife and daughter.

Nonetheless, however, one looked at it, our visit was something of a disaster through no fault of our own.

"Well, look here," announced the amiable gentleman, reaching for a jacket of impeccable checking, "I'd better run you home."

And so we exited, once more within the luxury of the Bentley, and soon found ourselves back at home, somewhat disorientated by the events so fresh in our minds.

During the journey to our trailer the father of the inebriated offspring offered us, to our astonishment, some explanation of his son's toxic condition and its effect upon both his school and family. He was apparently a pupil at one of the most renowned public schools – an establishment boasting the highest of moral codes, unwilling to countenance those who failed its standards. Thus, for the second time, the seventeen years old youth was ejected from its almost sacerdotal precincts – despatched by taxi to his family home wherein, it was hoped, curative inducements could be offered. That such could be achieved seemed to be viewed with some scepticism by his father. Himself, we later learnt, no stranger to the dubious charms of alcohol, which later took its toll upon him physically.

It was all very depressing to me, and we arrived back at our little trailer, fretting slightly at the inequalities of life aboard this planet.

The next morning, quite early, a police patrol-car stealthily drew up beside us and a hatless constable emerged, notepad in hand, features inexpressive.

After some questions as to our names and ages, and a check with his headquarters, he was satisfied that we did not feature on his 'wanted' listings. Nonetheless he insisted we should move despite our obvious non-effect upon nearby householders – of whom there were none.

Eventually, after considerable and logical arguments from myself he agreed that we could stay for the rest of the day, to give us time to try to single-out a landowner or farmer of amiable disposition who might suffer our presence on any spare ground or field for a week or so.

Leaving Beshlie behind, I set off on the difficult quest for a private stopping-place, or 'pull-in' as it is called by Travellers.

At that time, with the publication of '*Smoke in the Lanes*' no great distance behind me, I was wont in such circumstances, to introduce myself as a 'writer' in order to allay suspicion and, to the rustic mind appear nothing more than an eccentric. It was a ruse which worked on many occasions in those times: today I would never demean myself so.

After only two attempts I uncovered a pleasant and hospitable-seeming farmer who agreed to accommodate us in a nearby field for a week – charging me the princely sum to ten shillings, which I paid there and then.

The field, only an acre or so in size and a little spongy, was agreeably shielded from public gaze – private without being remote.

I hastened back to Beshlie with the good news and we were soon packed and on the road. The distance to be covered was no more than eight miles, which we achieved in less than half an hour. The gateway was of some twelve-feet wide, allowing us easy access from the road. Engaging four-wheel drive we sped over the damp surface with but little anguish – though with the lesser power of two-wheel drive we would undoubtedly have become bogged-down and immobilised.

Before evening I lit a small fire and we cooked ourselves a pleasing variety of vegetables, and rabbit, which we soon devoured with the hunger of youth, coupled with an appreciation of being able to afford even such humble fare.

A friend of mine from Bristol was at that time engaged in the collection of scrap bagging and sacks, from which industry he was securing a reasonable living.

Upon an impulse I decided, on the first day of 'calling' with the Jeep, to attempt the same, perhaps a little uninspiring, task; especially as we were in a rural area where such materials could be found by the diligent scavenger.

After several enquiries, met with flat refusals and no little hostility from both yeoman and rustic, I eventually made a lucky strike at a neglected looking farm.

In truth, the condition of the latter farmhouse and barns were so desolate that I almost avoided it.

It was extraordinarily old-fashioned I perceived. As I drove into the yard I was aware of half a dozen or more collie dogs, each chained to individual barrels and dotted around the yard. All were of considerable age, their stances unsteady, and their barks hollow and gruff: they did not give the impression of a happy life.

Hearing their geriatric barks a figure emerged from the front door. A man of some age, hunched and tubby, a dark velour hat on his head, and wearing an old ragged lounge-suit jacket, green corduroy breeches and worn-down brown boots: pride in his appearance seemed absent.

However, I was to be further surprised when he addressed me, his broad and pasty features suddenly contorted and he emitted a greeting of such volume that I jumped backwards in surprise.

"How be you, mister?" he roared, unaware of my shock. "What can I do for 'ee?"

"Well, I'm buying old sacks and bags – I wonder if you might have a few to sell me?"

"Gawd bugger, mister – I got half a shed full!" he shouted at full volume.

Hardly believing my shattered ear drums I nonetheless rallied in spirit.

"Come on along've I an' have a look at 'em," he suggested, with no moderation in sound.

Picking up a stick he walked over to one of the outbuildings with heavy, rotting, wooden doors, which he eventually pulled outwards. Utterly inexperienced in the purchasing of sacking or bags I was a little bemused by what confronted me. It was, in fact, a huge pile of rotting sacks, dust-filled and falling to pieces: it was, I rightly judged, 'sacking.' A spectacle which to anyone but the initiated, would be viewed as being without any value whatsoever.

I surveyed the mound with some disgust. Could it really have any commercial value? I could but hope.

After making several offers, each met with a blast of negation so great in volume that it surely must have wafted away to the nearest dwelling, a cottage of over a mile in distance.

Despite the uninhibited roars and shouts, however, we eventually settled on a figure which was acceptable to us both. It was scarcely a labour of love for me to load the fumy material onto the Jeep, and the eventual bulk was so great that it was necessary to secure the load with binder twine to avoid possible spillage on to the highway.

Once loaded, and after a thunderous farewell from the ancient rustic I set off to a neighbouring town wherein there was to be found a Sack and Bag Merchant, who was reputed to be a fair buyer and not averse to Travellers.

It was some ten or twelve miles to my destination and, once there, I had no trouble in locating the yard which lay in the High Street. Strangely enough the business was run entirely by its owners – a spritely couple of indeterminate age and restrained manner. The woman was clad in headscarf and fake-fur booties, her body encased in a ragged coat of geometric pattern scarcely designed for its present surroundings, whilst the man, cold blue eyes peering from beneath the peak of an excessively generous tweed cap, was attired in a dusty-looking brown 'smock' of the kind favoured by warehousemen.

They both stared in slight disbelief at myself and my rather unusual vehicle.

"Morning," I said cheerily. "I've got a bit of sacking here."

"Ar," observed the man, squinting. "Price ain't too good at the moment."

"Ar," I returned. "How much are you paying?"

With that he quoted me a figure, greatly in front of what I had given to the invisibly-megaphonic farmer: it was not too optimistic to feel that a Good Day was within my grasp.

Hence, after weighing the sacking on capacious scales my final reward was very heartening.

As is the custom with all dealers in 'scrap' they paid me in cash without subjecting me to the trials of paperwork or other extraneous details which, so often afflict even the simplest of business transactions.

It was soon after one o'clock that I returned to the field, flushed with triumph at my unexpected good fortune.

However, as is so often the case bad followed good. Hardly had we consumed our usual rough-and-ready fare when we observed the farmer driving across the field towards us in his battered Land Rover. I think that his expression could be described as a combination of embarrassment and unease: we sensed the purpose of his mission.

Indeed our qualms were not without foundation.

Descending from his Land Rover he awkwardly delivered his message.

"I'm sorry to say it, but I've had the Estate Manager over home this morning – an' raisin' hell he was about you being here – he says there's rules in my tenancy as to caravans – none's allowed on the Estate at all. He showed it to me, so what could I say?"

"That means you want us to go – right?"

"Well, I'm sorry, it does – there's nothing I can do about it. Course I'll give you your money back – here."

So saying he handed me back my ten-shilling note.

As I had paid in advance, and he had accepted the payment, I felt that we probably had a legal right to remain for the week. However, as those who have known it, eviction is extraordinarily dispiriting no matter what the circumstances.

And so it was that, at early light the next morning we were out of the field and on the road. Cowardly, possibly, but we decided once more to seek solace in the bosom of Fryern: a haven which, given the age of Augustus, could only last for a limited time, to take of advantage of occasional comforting circumstances should rarely be shunned, as they are all too infrequent in life.

Thus by midday we were once again ensconced within the boundaries of Fryern.

After pondering on the matter, and discussing it with a pleased Augustus, we decided to stay for the whole winter at Fryern. With sporadic modelling fees from the artist, coupled with efforts of my own, we felt confident that our survival could be achieved.

Our immediate aim was to sell the waggon, then the Jeep, and to dispose of our old trailer too – hoping to realise sufficient funds for us to buy a larger, later, model.

Our first transaction was the exchange of the Willys Jeep for a minute Bradford Jowett van. The latter, a vehicle of remarkably low power, its engine sounding like a sewing machine, was, however, capable of about sixty miles per gallon, yet with a capacious body. Incapable of towing a trailer, it was ideal for the occupation that I foresaw myself engaging in during the winter – namely that of 'antiques'. Its low cost of running would allow me to cover a wider area than possible with a larger horse-powered vehicle. It was also of no great age, being a 1952 vintage. Painted dark blue it assured me the kind of anonymity that I had hitherto not craved. Despite its sheer awfulness we nonetheless viewed it with affection – a reaction which surprised us both. From then on, as ever, things took unexpected twists.

Only two days after our acquisition of the Bradford Jowett I was surprised, upon returning home at midday to be met by Beshlie with the astonishing news that she had sold our trailer for a hundred pounds! From out of the blue a man and woman had stopped and asked if the trailer was for sale. It later transpired that the man had enquired at the local garage if he know of one and, knowing my propensity for buying and selling, had directed him to Fryern.

Beshlie learned from the prospective buyer, accompanied by a much younger female companion, that he had just emerged from prison with limited funds and was hence seeking accommodation of an accessible price.

Beshlie, always alive and responsive to unexpected situations, had wisely, closed the deal at one hundred pounds in cash. Rather rashly she had promised that it would be vacated in two days, presuming that, should all else fail, we could move back into the waggon until we found another trailer. It was a luxury to have such choices, and halcyon were such days – even though we did not fully appreciate it at the time.

A spark of memory stirred me into action in view of the urgency of the moment. I suddenly recollected having seen a trailer caravan standing, apparently unused, in the orchard of a well-appointed thatched dwelling within the bounds of the New Forest, an area sprinkled with such homes for the well to do. Suddenly I had the feeling that I might be able to purchase it, if it met with our requirements. I set out with high hopes and was soon knocking on the front door, the little Bradford parked nearby, its minute size still evoking much wonder in me.

The door was opened by an elderly, rather timorous gentlewoman. Upon my asking if she was the owner of the caravan she nodded her head daintily and said: "Oh no, it belongs to my niece Georgie who is in the stable over there." She pointed to a loosebox some little distance from the house, partially obscured by a new-looking sleek Vauxhall Estate, painted in a pleasing combination of contrasting pinks – a colour-scheme unlikely to find favour in the eyes of the average suburban driver, and destined to go out of production after a year or so.

I walked across as directed and was faced by a somewhat 'horsey' looking lady of middle years, complete with silk headscarf and cream riding breeches. She held a curry comb in her hand and was grooming a fine-looking chestnut hunter standing inside the box.

I introduced myself and apprised her of my quest.

Her features, long and heavily lined, were not unpleasant and indeed she seemed congenial.

"Hmm, I *might* consider it."

We walked through the orchard and I was able to inspect the trailer at close quarters. Although the exterior was a little green from its proximity to trees it was free of dents or other damage; also in its favour was the presence of a chimney projecting from the roof, happily denoting the inclusion of a solid-fuel stove. The latter was an item rarely shunned by Travellers until well into the 'eighties' when it was universally abandoned in favour of the less invigorating, but cleaner, 'bottled' gas.

Upon the name plate was inscribed 'Lisset' – a firm hitherto unknown to me. Inside the twenty-two feet body were the combined features of refined living: namely an end bedroom to the rear, and a central living room accompanied by large stove of the sort to be found in many a bungalow at that time. Whilst at the front end was a kitchen, with gas stove and sink, joined to a minute 'toilet' compartment, in which none but the most athletic could have performed anything other than the basic rites. The latter, however, was of no moment to us as Traveller-style, we would never consider its use for the purpose intended. There are limits to human degradation!

"I intended to let it in the summer," explained the amiable horsewoman. "But we decided that we didn't want strangers running all over the place," she added.

"Well, it would probably do for us – if you're not asking too much," I said, tentatively.

She smiled at me, lighting an expensive brand of filter-tip cigarette and offering one to me, which I accepted.

After a few inhalations she went on, "I gave three hundred for it – I wouldn't want to lose, so I'd take three hundred from you, which is not dear I'm sure."

"Well no," I agreed, "but I think I've only got two at the moment."

This was not strictly true but I could not help myself so I had to try.

"I could give you two hundred here and now, and pay the other hundred within two months."

"Oh dear," sighed the horsewoman, undecided as how to accept this turn of events.

"How about thinking about it, and I'll telephone you this evening," I suggested helpfully.

"Yes, all right. 'Phone me at about six, can you?" she replied.

With that I agreed and departed for home feeling confident that, one way or another, a deal would be accomplished.

Speeding along the narrow roads, the little engine somehow giving the impression of expanding in power from a sewing machine to that of a lawnmower, the ride was quite magical. It was best described as being a similar experience to that of transportation in a mobile hen-house.....but none the worse for that.

"Tch-tching" across the field I was met by Beshlie, and I soon explained the situation to her. We agreed that before finalising the deal it would be advisable for her to view the trailer too, lest its faintly unexciting interior fell below her wishes. At that point, of course, it was within the understanding of both of us that we were merely ascending the first rung of the ladder of ambition which was to be climbed steadily if we hoped for any respect from those engaged in the same lifelong pursuit.

I telephoned at six o'clock as arranged, and was told that a sale might well be negotiated. It was further agreed that we would meet the following morning to discuss it, also to give Beshlie an opportunity to cast a critical eye over the prospective home.

Starting out the next day at about nine thirty we found ourselves outside the orchard in which stood the object of our mission. Its very length seemed a little unnerving in the cold light of morning, but I dismissed such unacceptable fears at once. Nothing must halt our progress.

It was not long before we had enticed the horsewoman from the loose box and we entered the trailer. Eye contact between Beshlie and myself indicated that she was not wholly displeased by its layout, and that we should attempt to instigate a deal.

After some scarcely concealed doubts on the part of the vendor it was eventually agreed on my offer of two hundred pounds to be paid on collection, and a further hundred to follow within three months. The matter was completed there and then, a painless procedure.

Of course, having no motor capable of towing such a large trailer it would be necessary to engage the owner of a lorry for the task. Luckily, a Traveller friend of mine, one Caleb Smith, who had just arrived in the area, would undoubtedly help me out of the predicament. It was settled upon that the removal would take place within two days, giving us time to remove our belongings from our present trailer and stow them temporarily in the waggon, thus allowing the faintly sinister buyer and his lissom girlfriend to take possession and to tow it to whatever location they had secured.

Such was the paucity of our worldly possessions in those days that it was a matter of but a couple of hours before the trailer was empty, sad and naked like the carcass of a gutted and plucked chicken.

Upon completion of this labour of necessity I drove the 'hen-house' to a nearby telephone box and, with a number provided, spoke to the ex-prison inmate who appeared to be pleased that the trailer was ready to be re-located whenever he cared to do so.

It was then about four o'clock in the afternoon so I was not a little astonished when he announced that he would pick it up within the hour. Sure enough, and true to his word, the buyer arrived in an old Austin saloon car of 1939 vintage, one of the larger models generally procured by those in the Private Hire or Hackney Carriage occupation. In those days such vehicles could be bought for as little as fifty pounds or less. With heavy fuel consumption, and petrol at five or six *shillings* a gallon who could afford to run them?

In any event the buyer, grey-headed, shifty-eyed, and chain smoking, withdrew one hundred pounds from his trouser pocket and, with a wink, handed it to Beshlie who accepted it graciously. His youthful companion remained in the front passenger seat, a toothy smile disturbing her otherwise taut features. Young second wife, temporary girl-friend, trainee taxidermist? Who could tell?

With my assistance the trailer was soon affixed to the towbar and sat surprisingly level – though somewhat incongruously behind the stately limousine. Seeing the trailer being pulled out of the gateway and out of our life was a great relief. It had given me experience and earned me a profit from my initial outlay, thus it could not be heartily disparaged. Nonetheless we were pleased to see it go under such circumstances. Oh that all my future trailer-dealings had provided such profits.

Luckily the winter rains had not set in so the removal of the trailer from the orchard would not be overshadowed by the danger of it sinking in mud.

Caleb arrived the next morning in his Bull-nosed 30 cwt Bedford lorry, maroon in colour, lined-out in straw colour, with intricate traditional buckle-belt designs on each door, his initials nestling within them. A new heavy-duty 'step' drawbar completed its essentially 'Travellery' appearance. Alas, such badges of distinction were soon to disappear as the Age of Anonymity proved more advantageous in the field of business.

"Big old trailer, *mush*," observed Caleb when confronted with the 22ft Lisset. "Still, my lorry'll pull her easy, don't worry about that."

The horsewoman, on noting our presence strolled over, a mixture of curiosity and interest I presumed.

"Morning Madam," said Caleb, adding archly, "Nice day for it!"

He gave me a sidelong glance, winking cheerfully.

With the speed of a practised hand Caleb jacked-up the trailer ball-hitch and with unerring skill reversed his lorry's tow-bar exactly beneath it, and upon lowering the trailer jockey-wheel the fitting clicked into place. Thus, with all four 'legs' raised, he pulled gently forward and, with but a slight hesitation, we moved slowly across the orchard and on to the road. As the journey was quite short we did not bother with the formalities of either number-plate or rear light fixtures. In those day such things had not assumed the importance that is placed upon them today.

Happily it was no time at all before we were swinging round into the field entrance at Fryern, unhitching the trailer by the hedge, and enjoying a cup of tea by the *yog*.

"You can't beat a bit of fire an' a nice cup of tea outside," observed Caleb in customary Traveller appreciation of old-fashioned ways.

I thanked Caleb profusely and handed him the 'drink' that I had promised him for assistance.

He spat on the money and remarked, "I bet it won't be long 'fore you gets yourself a bran-fine new lorry – you gotta spend the *loover* , you cain't take it with you!"

"Huh! I wish I had your money, Caleb," I grinned.

"Cah! – Don't say that – I ain't a-got a shillin' 'cept what you give me just now. Old motors an' trailers've took every penny I had."

He was quite a well to do man, and he knew that I was aware of it.

As he was leaving, standing by his lorry, he brought my attention to his latest purchase. Pointing to the bonnet with some pride he showed me his *two* silver-plated horse-and-jockey mascots, one slightly ahead of the other as though in a race. Previously, and subsequently I had noticed the mascot as being a favourite amongst Travellers – but this was the first sighting of a twin arrangement that had caught my eye. It was indeed the last.

Sadly, today such embellishments have disappeared, partly by reasons of changes in the law, but mainly because, like most fashions, they were by-passed by time.

As Caleb was at that time earning his living practising what was known as 'the Showman's Tale' it was in his favour that his vehicle resembled, to the untrained eye, the aspect of the fairground ethos.

With some goodly revs and shouts of farewell Caleb was gone.

Horse-and-Jockey Mascots

Beshlie and myself set about flinging every moveable item from the trailer and then carried out the onerous labour of both washing and polishing walls, surfaces, and floors. In that pathetic task we hoped, as ever, to mould our surroundings to ourselves. It was almost dusk before we completed matters to our satisfaction.

The Lissett had come into our possession with the added benefit of an almost unused gas canister, designed to augment both the cooking and lighting facilities. In those days, before the denizens of trailers became both reliant and addicted to everything being electrically operated, gas lights were virtually a standard fitting. Their efficiency, however, was dubious, the mantles, the equivalent of a light bulb, were fragile and over-responsive to the slightest adjustment. Many indeed were the trailers sporting black and burned patches above the fearsome illuminants.

It was with some trepidation that Beshlie and I experimented with them on our first evening. However, after mantles collapsing in shreds or casting out devilish flames, we abandoned them in favour of two or three small storm lanterns, the only drawback being a pungent odour and the ever present danger of uncontrollable flames issuing forth from the maladjustments of the gas lights.

With the skill of Beshlie, and the inclusion of homely wall-hangings, it was not long before we had impressed at least a small part of our personal tastes upon what had previously been somewhat barren territory. In those times the specialist market for Travellers' trailers was hardly developed. Hence it was an almost universal practice for Travellers, especially those who had but recently vacated waggons, to buy almost any of the larger touring models that had been intended as *Gaujo* holiday accommodation – many being only partly insulated, some not at all. Of course, such refinements as double-glazing were undreamt of, and, as a result, windows poured with condensation and dampness spread through bedding and fabric. It was an unexpected tribulation, to be endured by many, ourselves included.

However, it was undoubtedly an upward step from our first trailer: the end-bedroom and separate kitchen were in themselves a novelty to us. The solid-fuel stove was an especial pleasure and, loaded to capacity, cast out sufficient heat to defeat even the condensation on the windows. It seemed at that moment that the winter before us might hold fewer discomforts than we had suffered hitherto: a hope to be treasured.

A *Kipsy* – traditional Gypsy basket

Chapter 5

A Struggle for a Shilling

It was purely by chance that I had become acquainted with the owner of a small shop in the New Forest area dealing in that somewhat elastic commodity – antiques. This was, in fact, a businesswoman of some astuteness, yet with a multi-layered personality.

The little shop was well-filled, showing great variety in its assemblage of goods, both in quality and value. The ample figure of the businesswoman was seated, like some portly idol, in the midst of the array, her garments an arresting combination of the domestic and the formal. We fell into conversation, making, perhaps, a strangely assorted trio. That was the beginning of a relationship which was to be maintained, if somewhat warily, for years to follow.

Being, however, a person with wide interests and with unswerving faith in her own potentialities, the businesswoman was unwilling to contain herself indefinitely within the bounds of small-time dealing – although she was admirably equipped to engage with great skill in that pursuit. Thus, to universal astonishment, she suddenly proclaimed herself a White Witch, announcing her intention of devoting herself to the strange rites of her calling. One can only hope that such conduct added greatly to the flames of glory which were surely already playing about her head! The latter event occurred towards the end of our business association it must be said. I am unsure of its culmination, and would not care to speculate.

Nonetheless, in our prime dealing days of that winter the businesswoman and myself enjoyed numerous mutually profitable transactions. For, very soon after our first meeting, I had agreed to endeavour to supply her with certain articles for which she had a demand. These were, I was pleased to learn, mainly 'outdoor' objects in the way of old garden ornaments, such as cast iron benches and chairs, stone figures, urns, vases, troughs, pedestals and wire-work, all of which were, and still are, readily saleable, and available to the diligent scavenger.

The little Jowett Bradford's economy of fuel consumption allowed me to comb the New Forest and its environs for many miles in all directions, as the fancy took me.

It was, of course, largely a new world for me, my efforts sometimes yielding unexpectedly high profits from the purchases I made. I usually aimed for elderly houses of good class, but fallen into decay – with occupants of the same description, who might be pleased to receive a few pounds for objects that no longer held much attraction for them. However, even when I did spot objects of the kind I was seeking it was by no means infrequent for the often taciturn owners to refuse point-blank to enter into any form of transaction – sometimes regretfully, and sometimes with fury, as though I was insulting them. It is undoubtedly a source of immense frustration to the freelance would-be buyer, whatever his field, to come up against the person who has just what he wants but refuses to sell it. (Those who have propositioned the 'Nice Girl of Portsmouth' may have experienced the same feeling!)

'Calling', as Travellers refer to it, or going 'on the knock' as some dealers say, can be a disheartening occupation for those of an ultra-sensitive nature, for one is all too often in contact with the least attractive side of human nature, seldom meeting any sympathetic consideration. Indeed, if I had as many five pound notes as times I have had doors closed in my face, I should be a wealthy man today! Of course, since every caller who wishes either to buy or sell something is invariably confronted with a 'No,' often before he has opened his mouth, he is unsurprisingly a little loathe to give this immediate negation his instant acceptance without trying anything further in the way of persuasion – for if he did he might as well sit at home all day for all the good he would do himself.

Only a few days previously I was calling not far from Romsey when I noticed a likely looking Victorian dwelling, standing aloof from its neighbours, and suitably neglected looking. Deciding that it felt 'lucky' I walked up to the side path of the house and was met with a latticed gate which I found to be padlocked. At that moment a middle-aged woman with a savage 'perm' and florid complexion, emerged from the back door and caught sight of me

"No! I've got nothing to sell, and I don't want to buy anything!" she announced in a hoarse voice, although I had spoken no word

"Thank you," I said placidly. "I was hoping to….."

"I told you once; I've got nothing to sell, and I don't want to buy anything!" she repeated severely, her unattractive countenance in no way improved by her irritable expression.

At that point my well attuned eye fell upon a rusty wire-work plant stand lying behind a wheelbarrow, obviously discarded and unused.

"Oh yes, thank you," I replied politely. Then, as if an afterthought: "I wondered if you would like to sell that old wire-work thing over by the wheelbarrow? I like it, and I'd give you five shillings for it."

"What do you mean?" demanded the woman, apparently not uninterested at the thought of five shillings.

"That old wire-work plant thing," I said, pointing it out to her.

"You don't want that, do you?" she enquired, glaring at me with suspicion.

"Well yes, I should like it – I'd give you five shillings for it," I reaffirmed.

"Huh! Give me the money, then," ordered this surprising woman.

I handed her two half-crowns and she fetched the plant stand over to the gate and presented it to me. She remained adamant that she had nothing further to sell so I left, with rather mixed reactions.

My spirits were lifted when, driving through Lyndhurst, I noticed a rather superior-looking 'Antiques Centre' beside which building lay a small enclosed yard displaying a fulsome collection of garden furniture. The owner proved to be of tractable disposition: a tall, dark, lantern-jawed person of inscrutable expression.

To any event, to my thinly disguised satisfaction, I was able to negotiate a deal with him that transformed my lower expectations into what an Old Devon Traveller was wont to call 'A Nice Little Day!' It was just luck – that rare commodity that is the goal of all those like-minded to myself!

During the weeks to follow, the businesswoman, with whom I was dealing almost exclusively, requested me to look out for stone troughs, of the sort which were once commonly used on farms, for which overstrainingly weighty objects she announced that she would be able to offer me up to twenty pounds each, depending on the size. Twenty pounds in those days when 'a pound was a pound' was an inspiring sum.

Upon the few occasions when I purchased really cumbersome and heavy troughs, the little Bradford Jowett suffered considerably, sometimes, when loaded, assuming a sit-up-and-beg position guaranteed to bring on nervous tension in the mind of any conscientious 'weights and measurers' man should he have happened upon us – which luckily did not occur.

I recollect when I was driving, one day, along a side road in the Purbeck country near to Swanage, hoping as ever for a lucky strike, when my glance fell upon a very cumbersome-looking stone trough lying beside a semi-derelict farmhouse, apparently no longer in use. I swung my little van across the road and parked beside the narrow gateway to the farmyard, in which I noticed two aged countrymen loading bales of straw on to a battered tractor-trailer. I walked over towards them, and they ceased their work and stared at me with a strange mixture humility, curiosity, hostility and suspicion – all expressions quite familiar to those in my position. They both wore dark blue dung-stained trousers and waistcoats, striped collarless shirts, pulled down caps, and hob-nailed black boots. One had a broad leather belt, low across the 'fly' of his trousers, worn with the silver buckle to one side.

"Morning," I remarked.

"What do 'ee want, then?" enquired the one wearing the low-slung belt, and both men squinted at me through pale grey eyes beneath their cap peaks, 'shushes' of white hair projecting out, identically, over their foreheads. Each had a half-smoked cigarette clamped to one side of their mouth.

"Well, I'll tell you what I want," I replied. "I wondered if you'd like to sell me that old trough lying over there?"

"Old trow?" repeated the beltless one, somewhat incredulously.

"Ar he mins thik old un what's led over be thik bit've shootin,'" explained the other.

"That's it," I agreed.

"What's 'ee worth to 'ee then, you?" asked the first man, and I knew then that I would be able to buy it.

"I tell you what I'll do – I'll give you ten shillings for it," I ventured.

"A half sovereign note! Fuck 'ee! Make it a sovereign an' you can take un on," said the belted one.

"I'll give you fifteen shillings," I countered.

"Ar take un on then, my cocker," he agreed, somewhat to my surprise.

"Will you give me a hand to load it into the van?" I requested.

"Ar, bugger, I bet he weighs all on four hundredweight, you," gauged the one in the belt.

"I'll fetch a coupla poles, you," announced the other.

Eventually he returned with two fairly long stout poles which we eventually managed to prise under the great trough so that their ends projected some four feet or more on each side of it.

The man in the belt took one pole end and I grasped the one next to him, whilst the first man, prouder and stockier than us, held both ends on his side of the trough, and with much straining, grunting, and cursing we succeeded in raising it from the ground and carrying it to the back doors of the Jowett. Whereupon, after a breather, we at length slithered the unyielding burden on to the bed of the little van, with just sufficient room to close the rear doors. It was an heroic achievement.

The journey back from the Purbecks was one fraught with some considerable tension, the fear of a tyre blow-out, or even the flooring giving way under the unaccustomed weight, all combined to breed doubts as to the wisdom of making such demands upon the suspension of the brave little motor. But, as they say, what could one do?

At that time I was in the habit of unloading all my 'finds' in a compact yard situated beside the shop of the businesswoman, after having been paid a price which had been settled upon. This particular trough, one of the heaviest that I had ever obtained, needed considerable effort to move it at all, but after much heaving the businesswoman, myself, and a passing gormless youth, proceeded to slide it down a plank – which, when the trough was halfway to the ground, suddenly splintered and collapsed, causing the enormous trough to land with a thud and a crack – in two separate halves, cleanly split! To her credit, on this and other occasions, even when I had hidden faults by covering them with mud, the businesswoman showed no malice, and we treated such incidents as a joke.

Sometimes perseverance bred good fortune. Once, when I had been out nearly all day and had found nothing worth attempting to buy, I was about to turn homewards, thoroughly dispirited, when I glanced into the garden of a house, standing on its own, which I happened to be passing, and instinctively pulled up. I walked up the drive, noticing as I did so that there was an old once-painted iron garden bench lying on its side by some bushes. It was not, alas, a Coalbrookdale but it was a not too inferior imitation. I knew it would be saleable, and I knocked on the front door, which was painted a calming shade of ochre.

It was opened by a young woman, with straight shoulder length hair, wearing a beige cardigan, infinitely muted plaid skirt, ankle socks, and brogues of immense practicality. Her face was of reasonable bone structure, although it did not have the benefit of any colouring, either natural or applied. Her expression, though not hostile, was earnest and serious. A small, shorn, pale skinned boy clung to her knee.

"What a funny man," remarked this perceptive child.

"Er, yes," I agreed, gazing with some dislike at the brat. The mother, in the way of her kind, did not reprimand it.

"Good afternoon," I said to her. "I am buying old scrap iron, and I wondered if you might have anything you want to get ride of – like old stoves or fireplaces or even that old seat over there – anything iron, you know?"

"Well, we haven't anything much," replied the woman. "But there's that old seat, and two chairs like it, only smaller, over behind that shed. What would you give me for them?"

I went over and glanced at the seat, and also the two chairs, which were of the same ornate design, discovering that although all were rusted and slightly damaged they were nonetheless quite repairable.

"Well! I'm afraid there is not very much weight in them, but I'll give you a pound for them," I replied, gazing sadly at the young mother.

She appeared very pleased with the offer, accepting the pound note with alacrity as though fearing I might change my mind.

Loading my purchases into the rear of the little Bradford Jowett I drove on. After a mile or so, descended a steep incline, I found myself in the middle of a very genteel looking village, of the sort which seems to develop quite suddenly these days, where most of the genuine country people are living in groups of council houses, whilst the thatched and similarly picturesque dwellings, expensively modernised and extended, are occupied by 'County' types, imitation County, or the folksy.

I parked outside an obviously newly 'improved' thatched cottage to gather my wits, marvelling at the mixture of repulsive modern gnomes and other statuary which were scattered about the garden – not that the inhabitants would have wished to sell them, nor I to buy. I left the van and bought two tins of evaporated milk from a small shop opposite. I was just about to start the engine when I was shaken out of my reverie by a loud cry. Turning round in the driver's seat, and leaning out of the window I beheld a strange figure peering into the rear windows of the van.

"Ahaaaaaaa! I say! Can I have a word with you?"

The speaker was a woman unsubdued by her advancing years, tall yet rather ungainly in movement, wearing a brown beret, sheepskin coat, and a very hairy skirt, bald in places, of rough-hewn weave, accompanied uneasily by green wellington boots. Yet about her was that almost indefinable air of refinement which sometimes presents itself in the most unlikely looking persons.

"Good afternoon, how can I help you?" I said, sensing the possibility of an advantageous encounter.

"Ahaaaaaaa!" she squawked, in what proved to be a characteristic prefix to most of her utterances.

"Damned cheek, I suppose, but are you an antique dealer – only I noticed those garden seats and wondered if you want to sell them?"

93

At that point she was joined by an aged Labrador, chocolate coloured and of uncertain docility, indeed, it broke into a sporadic burst of croaking barks on sight of me.

"Quiet, Major," commanded the gentlewoman querulously.

I was naturally slightly amazed by the opportunity of a sale falling so unexpectedly into my lap.

"Well, I am going to sell them, but I've got a dealer in antiques who is specifically interested in this kind of thing so he always gives me a good price."

"Ahaaaaaaa! I see, oh dear, yes. And how much do you think you would get for them?" cried this unnerving person, her short grey hair glistening like a badger's beneath the beret.

"I should get at least fifteen pounds for the two chairs, and about forty for the bench," I replied calmly, testing the water.

"AHAAAAAAA1" screeched my potential buyer in a storm of what I realised was a slightly affected reaction. "You rogue!" she cried, the faintest hint of jocularity passing swiftly over her leathery countenance.

"I am *not* a rogue," I asserted, staring seriously at her.

"Yes, you *are* a rogue – I can see it in your eyes – an absolute rogue! Fifty five pounds indeed. Pah! I'd give you thirty, even though you are a rogue!"

I found myself warming to this ebullient old person. Giving way to any personal feelings, as a dealer, is frowned upon by those in the profession. For me, however, it is a luxury that I sometimes allow myself.

"What they say is; One bidder is worth fifty lookers-on," I replied with a smile.

Both dog and prospective buyer gave me the benefit of their respective stares.

"I'll tell you what I will do," I remarked amiably. "I'll take forty pounds for the three."

"Ahaaaaaaa! You rogue!" cried the gentlewoman, at even higher volume. "I'll give you thirty-five for the three – and not one penny more!"

It was an offer, in the monetary values of time, too good to refuse.

Thus, within minutes I had off-loaded them in the back garden of her nearby house, a Georgian property of some majesty, as befitted the widow of a retired Admiral, knighted and be-medalled, as I later learned.

It was not our last encounter. Some months later we came face to face in the market place at Salisbury. As it happened we were unable to conduct much of a conversation as, nearby, a lunatic had erected a wooden stage some six feet tall. From this platform he was delivering a startling harangue at top volume through an ear wrecking megaphone. The message, although loud, was not fused into any form of logic. With his perplexing doctrines and desperate expression, one could not help but feel that one was listening to a message from Grimms Fairy Tales – from someone on speed!

The Admiral's widow was, to my delight, outraged by this intrusion into the aural privacy of the market-place. Urged by her to accost the speaker and request that he diminish the volume, I approached the demented megaphone-holder and gestured to him encouraging him to descend and speak to me.

This he did, a wispy-haired, unhinged looking man in his forties, I judged.

Upon receipt of my request for him to discontinue disturbing the peace his face became distorted with indignation and righteousness.

"I am here," he assured me, "doing the Lord's work and telling of the Heavenly Path that we must follow in order to give ourselves up to the love of the Lord Jesus. Amen. I will *not* stop my work – and you, in the Devil's pay, will remember this on the Day of Judgement!"

Alas, lunacy, in whatever form it takes, is largely non-combatable, I fear.

Upon relating the result of my mission, and the 'preacher' having resumed his lofty position, the redoubtable lady, demonstrating that the spirit of Empire-building had not perished, announced her intention of repairing to the nearest police station to issue a strong complaint, and a plea for noise abatement.

We parted amicably and I resumed my patrol around the market stalls.

On my departure I was forced to pass by the religious maniac, still in full spate despite an unresponsive audience. However, my delight could barely be constrained when I beheld the admiral's widow, accompanied by middle-aged helmet wearing constable, in animated conversation with the self-styled preacher. The latter's face was, one could see, puce with self-righteous indignation; but it was obvious that in the figures of her ladyship and the constable, each inhabiting their own time zone, he could expect nothing but defeat. Tool of 'The Dear Blessed Lord' or not the megaphone would have to go! The forces of urban law and order would prevail.

That winter was my heyday in the garden furniture market, before it began to pall, and many indeed are the memories that I have of cold dark afternoons, driving the little Bradford Jowett back across the open spaces of the New Forest, chilly with no heaters in those more Spartan motoring times, speeding in an effort to reach the businesswoman's shop before it closed. One very great advantage of dealing with the businesswoman almost exclusively was the fact that she was willing to buy virtually anything that I offered her, and did not pick and choose like a vicar's wife, rooting out the good from the bad. Also she was not above assisting me unloading from the van herself when no one else was available, her heavily be-ringed hands showing an unexpected strength. She would also appreciate my shameless habit of accosting the first man who happened along, no matter what his social status, and attempting to enlist his help in the removal of heavy, often mud covered objects from the van. Even greater amusement was afforded us by those who tendered singularly unlikely excuses as to why they could not do so – frequently gazing at us with the disbelief of one who suddenly finds himself drawn unexpectedly into a private game of charades.

It is to me, and almost all Travellers, a matter of pride and status to be self-employed even though denied the security of a regular income. Of course, the saying goes: you'll never get rich on wages.

Undoubtedly there are moments when those never-ending uncertainties of 'calling' can be mentally and physically exhausting and it is necessary to fall back upon reserves of stamina and determination in order to keep going. Sometimes I have called solidly for two or three days in succession, no matter what my mission, without earning a penny. It is then that one's resilience as a survivor is tested to the utmost: it is there that Travellers excel and determination invariably wins through.

By the middle of March, however, spring had made a welcome appearance; warmer weather, longer days, and all nature awakening around us. It was, I felt, time for both a move and a change of direction. As ever fortune intervened, this time in the shape of two gay grocers in the nearby town – in whose well-stocked little commissariat I was wont to exchange the kind of banter hardly likely to be favourably countenanced within the portals of the majority of Tesco's of today. In any event these two friendly shopkeepers were relating the demise of their faithful 1938 Austin Seven delivery van – its 'big ends' apparently beyond repair. Thus, as one would expect, I immediately suggested that they purchase my little Bradford Jowett. The suggestion was met with faint suspicion from the elder of the two, his waxy features assuming a look of caution. His friend, younger and slightly more glossy, blonde hair combed into a kind of pre-Elvis quiff, received my offer of a test drive with a reaction only just short of enthusiastic. Hence, within minutes, we were, by Bradford standards of pace, speeding out into the country – the little engine emitting its customary whines, ticking, and whirrs in unison as we eventually reached speeds approaching forty miles an hour, though within the confines of the vibrating body-shell it seemed faster.

The young looking grocer, entrepreneur of the delivery branch of the partnership, allowed himself a faint smile of arch-browed approval.

"Nice little mover," he observed.

"And the van," I replied, in a way that I knew would meet his approval.

"We'll have to see what Walter thinks," he said, apparently not wishing to make any decision without consultation, which seemed reasonable to me.

We were soon back outside the shop, Walter emerging on sighting us.

"How does she go?" he enquired.

"Oo, like a rocket!" declared his friend, to my relief.

"Well, come in," said Walter, his small eyes showing a hint of friendliness at the situation.

"What year is it – and how much are you asking?" he continued.

I apprised him of the year, and suggested £125 as the price, giving myself, as ever, a little room for manoeuvre.

They looked doubtfully at each other and I feared that I might lose them. Although in trade, as it were, they were neither of them by nature dealers which was a mixed blessing.

"It's a lovely little vehicle," I said, encouragingly. "I've not had a bit of trouble with her," I continued truthfully, adding: "But I've got to get a bigger one to pull my caravan."

They stared wordlessly at me.

"She'll run all day on a gallon of petrol – does sixty miles on it," I went on. "You'd never find a cheaper motor to run. Be just ideal for what you want – she's even got a bigger body than your old Austin Seven."

"We're a bit short of money just now," explained the younger man, apologetically. "I don't think we could manage £125."

I minded the old saying: You can always go down, but you can't go up.

"I'll try to help you here," I remarked. "Could you manage £105?"

They brightened slightly and Walter, to my surprise, replied: "Would you take £100 cash for it?"

A moment of affected pondering, then a ready assent from me. The deal was done and I agreed to deliver the van next morning, when they assured me that my cash would be awaiting me. In retrospect so little could buy so much, but of course, it was as hard in those days to earn £100 as it is to earn £2000 today.

And so after such a painless and unexpected transaction we regretfully parted with our first, and last, Bradford Jowett, an admirable little workhorse, then available in van or truck form – now, alas, long since out of production, like almost every one of those small and adventurous car makers each with a character of their own.

True to their word the rotund Walter, and his more elegant partner, were waiting for my arrival, one hundred pound notes clasped in the pudgy hand of the older grocer. I accepted the money both gracefully and gratefully. I felt it would be out of keeping to offer them any traditional 'luck' money back – as would have been the case had I been dealing with a Traveller.

In any event, to the best of my knowledge I had sold them a sound and reliable little vehicle, pretty enough to bring a sparkle to the eyes of all but the most morose of their customers.

I walked back to Fryern in thoughtful mood.

In earlier days to be without a horse was unthinkable and now the same could be said of being motor-less. It was akin to amputation.

My next vehicle was a two ton Austin lorry of 1948 vintage. It had suffered a life of unremitting toil, having been in the hands of a jobbing builder;a rather rough-hewn man, apparently with few talents, and fewer still in the art of constructions, his brick walls being notorious for their leanings and lack of longevity, whilst his attempts at roof-repairs never failed to lose the battle with the elements. Disgruntled clients were wont to complain. "If it didn't leak much when we called him in, then it was like a colander when he left!"

At the time there was a rumour that commercial vehicles over but few years in age would be required to undergo an annual test. This struck fear into the hearts and minds of those owners who had hitherto followed a path of neglectful optimism in regards to the mechanical status of their lorries. Thus, it seemed to them, the time of reckoning was at hand. It was inconceivable to them that they would be willing to pay for, what appeared to them, unnecessary repairs.

My encounter with such a builder enabled me to buy the rather beaten-up Austin for £17.10s! It was petrol driven, noisy, and lacking in any form of comfort for either driver or passenger in its rather cramped cab.

However, after a thorough repainting by Beshlie and myself it displayed a kind of broken-down attraction. It was like an old battle-scarred Game Bird, still functioning but well past its prime.

I taxed it for three months, as was possible then, as a Private vehicle for the sum of £3.10s, so we were, at least partly, quite legal – so long as we did not carry goods 'for reward.'

We kept it for three months, its capacious body lending itself splendidly to the accommodation of scrap-iron; a heavy task without more than poverty returns on most days; but it was a living of sorts.

Although the collection of scrap-iron has been an occupation which I have followed sporadically over the years its exhausting labour, and frequent fluctuations in the price paid by the owners of scrap-yards, has invariably been the cause of my abandoning it in favour of less arduous, and more rewarding, pursuits.

In the case of the Austin lorry it lasted for three months before its attraction palled. In this instance it was an easy decision, greatly accelerated by the owner of an agricultural contracting business offering me £35 for the lorry –its roomy body being ideal, he thought, for transporting hay and straw bales. As the profit was a hundred per cent it could not be refused.

The next day I engaged the services of Gilly Gayle to drive me over to Poole in Dorset. Just outside that town was a large 'car front,' owned by two brothers, second-generation settled down Travellers who always had a goodly stock of commercial vehicles at hand. I decided, after a telephone call, to purchase my next motor from them.

Gilly arrived at nine o'clock the next morning, his little van filled with the enticing odours of both a fish-and-chip shop and a municipal rubbish dump, the pervasive qualities of which he seemed unaware; an indifference possibly fostered by his non-stop inhalation of Capstone Full-Strength cigarettes.

After a journey of about half an hour, the van coughing ominously on any uphill gradients, we finally arrived outside the well-stocked 'car front' of Hillyer Bros.

Numerous gaudy placards were in evidence, some extolling the quality of the motors on display, others offering IMMEDIATE CASH for ANY vehicles, regardless of age or condition. The temptation was not for the faint-hearted.

I noticed that the commercial section was to the right of the clearly marked Office, inside which two shadowy figures were invisible. Upon sighting the dishevelled figure of Gilly, and myself, the office door opened and out came one of the Hillyer brothers. He was a man of perhaps forty years, grey-haired, and of unmistakeably Romani features, his face both lined and tanned. From the head down, however, he was the picture of a successful business man. His double-breasted suit, white stripes shining on a dark background, was tailor-made, whilst his foulard silk tie enjoyed a reciprocal marriage with a neatly striped shirt. His black shoes were narrow and expensive, a town-dweller's footwear.

He smiled a greeting and lit a filter cigarette, steadying it with a hand enriched by the presence of a broad gold ring, a diamond of considerable brilliance inserted in it.

We wandered down the line of lorries and vans until I caught sight of an unusually stream-lined 30 cwt Bedford van, of the A-Model variety. Painted a curious fudge colour, though not without a number of dents and scrapes, its unusual body construction appealed to me.

Further investigation and questioning of Bob Hillyer as to its ownership revealed that it was of 1953 vintage and had originally been owned by Uriah Burton the renowned Romani fighting-man who had used it in his carpet selling days. 1953 was the year when the first A-model was produced – a rather bulbous design, with a small windscreen and spacious cab. Like all 30cwt Bedfords, from the Bull Nose through to the 1959 J-type, its first gear was exceedingly low – allowing it to pull even heavy trailer-caravans up and over almost any gradient with which they were faced. They almost all, up until the 1960's boasted petrol driven engines. Later, of course, as diesel engines were developed and refined, petrol was abandoned in all mid-to-heavy trucks, the greater economy and efficiency of diesel becoming universally acknowledged.

Inspection of the registration book proved that the Bedford van had passed through many hands – a fact which *should* have deterred me from any further interest. However, an assortment of ignorance and wilfulness prevented my taking the sensible path.

"Can I hear her running?" I enquired. (At least I would know whether it would start, I mused.)

"Sure you can – I'll just fetch the key," replied the seller, and disappeared into the office, to reappear moments later, smiling, the all-important ignition key in his hand.

"She's bin standing, mind," he warned.

Insertion of the key, however, resulted, after two pulls on the self-starter, in the powerful 6-cylinder engine struggling into life. Familiar, to me, was the emission of blue smoke from the exhaust – a sure warning of excessive oil consumption. In those times, of course, I veered towards dismissive optimism, no matter what the evidence.

A short 'test drive' proved her to be capable of movement in a forward direction, even if rather lackadaisically, whilst the steering efficiency was in some way impeded by its apparent unwillingness to forego an independence of its own, bearing only a spasmodic reaction to the steering wheel, which made for adventurous journeys.

When I asked the price the younger Hillyer brother's eyes narrowed and he observed:

"Well, she's a tidy old motor – got plenty of life in her yet. Uie had that body made special to his likings."

"How much?" I asked again.

"A ton an' a half," he replied.

"A ton and a half?" I repeated, shocked of expression.

"I'd offer you a hundred pounds, and take a chance," I suggested.

"Best come in the office an' have a chat to me brother," he advised.

We entered the office, the malodorous Gilly at heel, and perceived the elder brother, Jack, seated at a desk. He did not have the pleasing attributes of his younger brother.

Short, heavily built, and faintly toad-like in demeanour, little affability emanated from him at first glance. His eyes, small and black as a rodent's regarded me inscrutably from his sallow face. His hair was a dense black but had been robbed of its freedom by over-application of peculiarly pungent pomade, and lay dispiritedly across his skull.

"Here's a young man come here to try an' diddle us," explained Bob, smilingly to his brother.

Jack unbent a little, lighting a large cigar and puffing contentedly without offering one to either myself or Gilly.

"He's trying to buy that Bedford van what Uie had the body made for – offered me a ton, he has. How can we take that?"

"A ton! Blessed God Above," said Jack mournfully. "If I took your ton I'd be losing money," he declared, straight of face. "I could sell motors all day if I didn't mind losing money – but what's the good of that? He's marked up at one and a half, which is cheap. But seein' as you're here I tell you what I'll do, I'll take one hundred and forty pound notes. That's the best I can do, young man."

"I can't do it," I said, regretfully. "I'll give you a hundred and twenty pounds, here and now – it's all the money I've got with me."

Jack glanced at Bob, who remained non-committal, and puffed on his cigar, a caricature of the late Lew Grade.

"Don't matter if you ain't got all the poke with you," he asserted. "We'll trust you for the rest."

"No thank you, I couldn't do that. I tell you what I'll do, and it's the best I *can* do, I'll give you one hundred and twenty-five pounds here and now and drive her away."

We all knew that an impasse had been reached. But I realised that if they accepted my offer they would still be in the golden land of profit: I gauged that they had probably paid about seventy pounds or less in a trade auction. They were famously clever men.

"You'd have to get up early in the morning to catch one of they," said a business associate of theirs to me one day.

"Let's have your bit of poke, then," said Jack finally, a look of affected gloom playing about his unattractive features: I took an instant liking to him, and slightly less so, to his brother. Their road must have been hard, their undeniable success was to be greatly admired.

And so, within less than half an hour, I was at the wheel of the Bedford and heading for home, leaving Gilly to follow me closely, lest disaster might strike at one or other of the two vans.

In retrospect it was probably the worst motor that I ever acquired, utterly lacking the 'charmed life,' whilst in my hands, of any of our other purchases of elderly worn-out vehicles.

Once at home in the field at Fryern it was clear to me that evidence of the van's 'rough passage' was even more apparent than I had suspected. Alas, my usual clear-sightedness had sadly deserted me. However, it was no time to cry – I had only myself to blame for such a misjudgement.

But, of course, the psychological damage had been done: it was, to me at any rate, an unlucky motor from the start.

The next day I drove to a small carpet factory near to Swindon and, persuading the owner that I was a legitimate shop-owner, I managed to negotiate a 'trade' purchase of a collection of singularly unattractive Belgian mats, repulsive enough in design to appeal to the undiscerning buyer, who one hoped might be attracted by their garish colouration. The latter did indeed, to my slight surprise, prove to be the case: I hawked them around council houses and was grateful to the denizens for relieving me of the entire consignment within two days. My pockets, though not strained, were comfortably immured by the presence of copious numbers of pound notes.

Yet despite my comparative success as a rug hawker, I found that I was uneasy in its grip. Council estates were not my favourite areas of calling, too many inhabitants facing financial straits almost as uncertain as my own.

However, fate was, as always, to take a hand.

I decided to engage in one of my favourite occupations: that is to say the lopping of small trees, trimming shrubs, and even hedges of no great substance. The results of such not too strenuous labour often proved quite exhilarating. That at least was my intention.

And so, cruising through a suburb of Bournemouth the next morning, I was pleased to see two young Travellers, friends of mine, resurfacing a driveway with tarmacadam. A brand new sky blue 30cwt Bedford lorry containing hot tarmac was standing outside the gateway and they were off-loading the tar into a wheelbarrow, a petrol driven roller standing ready to compress the raked out surface with the force of its vibrations.

They were brothers Nelson and Liberty Belltower, still on the roads with trailer-caravans, though most of their relatives had bought their own places and settled down in Hampshire and Sussex.

Black-haired and dark of complexion they were undeniably Romanies, but their manner was cheerful and polite to their customers and their skills in the laying of tarmac could not be faulted – smooth and pristine. Different indeed from the results sometimes achieved by less particular workers, whose inability even to approach such standards was frequently the cause of outcries from discontented householders.

It was the era of The Tarmac and The Trees.

The Belltowers were really Boswells, but their father had, in his younger days been imprisoned for fighting in a public house, during the course of which he had bitten off his opponent's left ear!

Upon completing his sentence he had assumed his new name, hoping to dissociate himself from his previous persona. From then his life took a series of upward spirals, culminating in him accruing enough money to buy two separate mobile-home parks, in which he installed *Gaujo* tenants of placid temperaments, and from the rentals of which he and his wife Phoebe enjoyed a comfortable income. Once known to them their hospitality and good humour were unrivalled – both long gone now of course, but their sons live on, almost all, seemingly, prospering in the way of their father; a continuity that is something to be envied by those of us not having such sturdy roots.

"Hi, Nelson," I greeted the elder brother, and smiling at Liberty.

"Where's you stopping?" he said, asking the customary question.

I told him, and they both grinned.

"Oh! Dordi!" laughed Nelson. "He's got himself in with that old *Rai* over by Fortinbree – he won't never shift."

"Huh! I tell you what, I'm shifting this week," I assured them.

103

"Where you stopping, Nelson," I asked.

"Over agen Romsey – in a farmer's field. We pulled there on Sunday. Why don't you come over for a week or two? I knows I can get the old farmer to let you in cos he's greedy for money. Shall I ask him?"

It was a nice gesture, and I felt happy to take advantage of it.

"Well, thanks Nelson – I'll pull over on Wednesday if he'll let us in."

"Yeah, okay," said Nelson, adding: "Here I'll give you the phone number of the *Kitchema* (public house) we uses. Ring up about eight o'clock tonight. We ain't big drinkers, you knows that."

And so it was arranged, the evening phone call bringing the good news that we were welcome – at a rent of only two pounds a week.

I went over to announce our departure to Augustus that evening and found him as usual at his desk, the usual box of one hundred Woodbines to his left hand and a newly opened bottle of Beaujolais on his right.

He welcomed me warmly, not too surprised at my leaving, as previously we had never stayed for more than two or three weeks. He accepted my ways.

Thereupon, after several glasses of red wine, and some agreeable reminiscences by Augustus, most concerning his bohemian life in Dorset in the 'twenties and 'thirties, which were both entertaining and enlightening, I took my leave – with the promise of a return within six weeks in order that he could continue his work on the portraits of Beshlie.

Hooking on the trailer to the van the next morning made me realise the frightening length of our combined turn-out. A more alarming prospect that I had been faced with up till that moment. However, knowing the number of Travellers in the same position, many with even less driving experience than myself, prodded me into a slightly apprehensive confidence. An alternative option was not available.

The route I chose was one of main roads in view of the cumbersome nature of our mechanised equipage, so we headed for Ringwood and then across to Romsey. The field we sought was, in fact, just past Romsey, on the way to the interestingly named King's Somborne. Nelson and Liberty had assured me that the trailers were visible, on our left hand side, about two miles along that road. In fact, and to my slight surprise, this proved to be the truth. As we arrived in mid- morning there was no one at home, the men out working on their tarmac contracts, and the women shopping.

Nelson and his brother were both young, not long married, and both fiercely embattled in the perpetual struggle to improve one's possessions. The need for the renewal of their trailers for models of more splendid design every year or two was paramount in the 'show-off' world of the so-called 'flash' Travellers. The same course was applicable to their lorries and private cars. Unlike some people, who affect to find such behaviour despicable, I can see nothing to despise – rather do I admire it. Indeed, I can go so far as to admit that it is a path which I have endeavoured to follow myself with varying degrees of success! For those of us in such a latitude it is always necessary to make not just a living, but a 'living-and-a-half." The 'half' being the amount put aside for the replenishment of our ageing chattels. The latter, be they trailers or motors, are generally absorbed by the less wealthy Travellers – usually disparagingly referred to as 'Rough Travellers' by their unsympathetic brethren.

It is a far cry from the old fashioned idea of The Romany Life as described with varying degrees of accuracy by so many writers, both of the past and present. However, it is the Romany people's ability to adapt themselves that has been their strength, and which will, one hopes, allow them to retain their ethnic identity.

We had hardly settled in when the two women arrived home in a smart salon car, painted in the fashion of the time, in two-toned blue.

It was Nelson's wife 'Melia, carrying their baby son, Nelson, and Liberty's wife Mary-Anne, so far childless – despite Liberty's assurance to me that he was doing his utmost to remedy that situation.

They were, in fact, sisters, both very handsome with sparkling black eyes and ringletty dark hair. Their clothes were bright and new, and their high heeled footwear ill- suited to the muddy field.

It was, and still is, a common practice for two brothers of one family to marry two sisters of another family and travel about together. Quite often, if they settle down, they will inhabit adjoining chalets, or even houses, so the togetherness continues. It is something that I have often envied.

Both 'Melia and Mary-Anne (known as Minna) were, besides being very good looking, exceptionally talented singers both as soloists or as a duet. Their presence at Travellers' parties was always a cause for celebration, such was their fame within the confines of their own society. Both were of bubbly and resourceful personality. They were from a large family, mostly outgoing and gregarious, generous spirited and cheerful. They were good company.

In between tarmacadam laying the brothers would sometimes engage in the simpler task of either 'tar and chippings' or even just 'chippings'. The latter form of surfacing for driveways was occasionally favoured by those householders with social pretensions, who sought the 'reserved' effect created thus. The colder, more clinical tarmacadam shunned, quite rightly in my opinion, for the preference of the quasi-rustic atmosphere of the golden shingle.

I unerringly homed in in this apparently uncomplicated profession with little hesitation.

The brothers generously provided me with the nearest location of a gravel merchant, from whom they were able to fill their lorries for the very reasonable sum of ten shillings.

The only complication being that it was necessary to drive one's lorry under a kind of chute, operated from above by a lever. There were four or five such chutes alongside each other and offering a variety of chippings, sized for choice from about a quarter of an inch, known as 'pea-grit' up to one or even two inches, 'pea-grit' or half-inch being the most popular sizes.

At that point I performed what must have been one of the most eccentric acts of my life. To the astonished amusement of Nelson and Liberty I seized upon a hack-saw and proceeded to cut a three feet square hole in the roof of my battered van, thereby enabling me to load it with the chippings from the gravel-pit chute. Such was my confidence that I persuaded myself that the ends would justify the means, which to some extent they did.

Arriving at the weighbridge the next morning I was confronted by a slightly dazed operator, who when told of my van's unexpected aperture in its roof rolled his eyes, in the manner of one for whom the world had few surprises left to offer him.

He weighed the empty vehicle, ready for him to re-weigh it before I left, laden with the gleaming chippings. Faintly above the sum quoted by Nelson I was nonetheless happy to pay the twelve shillings demanded.

Invention, dedication and determination must bring some reward, I felt sure. As ever, there was no alternative to optimism.

On the outskirts of Southampton I came upon some likely 'calling,' finding myself in an area made up of both oldish houses and newish bungalows – a catholic choice awaited me.

Keeping my eyes alert I espied a narrow, weed infested footpath beside a shabby dwelling, some fifteen or twenty feet long, leading to the back door. I left the van and knocked loudly on the bungalow front door. It was answered, to my surprise, by an elderly man with a stubby white face and what appeared to be a colourful tea-cosy as a casual headgear. He had, I supposed, some form of artistic pretension. But for the moment I was intent on the job in hand. He seemed quite attuned to the idea my suggestion that my attentions could greatly improve the neglected aspect of his footpath. Veering into the realms of fantasy I assured him that I would remove the weeds, and ensure their not returning by judicious application of a controlling substance which I spontaneously named as 'Thraxide.'

Asked the price I would charge, I suggested the sum of ten pounds, to include the 'weedkiller.'

After but a moment's hesitation this very 'easy' man said, "Right, well carry on –ring the doorbell when you've finished. I shall be in my studio."

Despite my condemnation of the Uie Burton's Bedford as being unlucky I could not deny that it had proved the opposite when confronted with my newest venture. To obtain a job from the first door upon which I had knocked was indeed a triumph in itself.

After spending about half an hour scraping off the weeds with a shovel, and scattering the diluted contents of a tin of evaporated milk, which I found in the cab, in a calculated conscience-appeasing gesture, about the footpath's length, I proceeded to spread the chippings in fluid gestures from a wheelbarrow borrowed from Liberty. Unaccustomed as I was to the amount required to cover such an area, I found myself astonished at how little had actually been needed to afford an adequate dressing. I was also encouraged at its appearance, bright, light, level and pristine. I was almost proud of my skill!

Before I had rung the bell to announce my completion the door was opened by the bungalow dweller, still in his tea-cosy and with a half smoked cigarette in his mouth.

He presented me with two five pound notes and offered me a cup of tea, which I accepted partly out of a curiosity about the interior of his home.

We went into a room facing out on to the back garden. It appeared to double as a kitchen and a 'studio': cooking appliances, crockery, sink and cupboards all arranged on one side, whilst an easel and other accoutrements of an artistic inclination were amassed in some confusion at the other. Slightly amazed at the unexpected sight I was further disconcerted to perceive that instead of tubes of oil paint or water colours there were countless tins of Japlac enamel, which, it appeared, engendered his creative artistry. Upon the wall there were several of his works, each enjoying the company of heavy, dark frames, the like of which would have killed less jubilant paintings.

Reflecting the primitive qualities of the Cornish artist Alfred Wallis and the impasto technique of Matthew Smith (a difficult feat to accomplish with Japlac without the addition of putty) their dramatic impact, unexpected in such surroundings, caused me to inhale in wonder. Lest their viewers were at a loss as to their actual subjects each picture was enhanced by the presentation of a title, in rough lettering, at the top.

Thus a wind tossed fishing boat was inscribed 'Storm at Sea', whilst a be-crowned and regal looking lady was 'H.M. The Queen.' All followed in that vein – perhaps the least successful being the depiction of a small mongrel dog protruding from an elaborate kennel, entitled, alas, 'In the Dog House.'

I left after about half an hour, having inspecting numerous of such creations, my senses dulled to the point that I could not decide whether I had discovered a future hero in the art world or whether, as I finally decided, creation does not always equate with actual talent. For over fifty years I have periodically questioned my decision, speculating that I might have become the agent of an undiscovered genius.

In order to recover I stopped outside a rather gloomy transport café called 'Joe's Place.' Upon entering I found myself in an atmosphere of cigarette smoke, stale fat, and sizzling fry-ups of a strongly noxious odour. The latter, one felt, could only be devoured with pleasure by those of a ravenous disposition. Nonetheless, the owner appeared friendly.

"All right, cock?" he greeted me, with an endearing wink.

"So far so good," I replied. "Can I have a bit of bacon, semi-cremated, tinned tomatoes, beans, and brown toast?"

"We ain't got no brown toast," replied the amiable Joe, with no hint of apology."

I collected a mug of strong tea and went to a plastic topped table to await my victuals.

I had scarcely sat down when, with a noisy entrance, three local Travellers came in. Glancing outside I could recognise their vehicle at once: a dark blue 30 cwt Bull-nose Bedford lorry, maybe seven or eight years old.

It was Big Bob, a mountainous figure of twenty stone or more, and his two brothers-in-law Dinky and Freddy. They were a curious trio, yet all of one mind in their desire to obtain employment from the unwilling residents of suburbia, either in the field of tarmacadam or tree surgery.

"How's your luck, kid?" enquired Big Bob, as they sat down at the table adjoining mine, each lighting a cigarette and inhaling deeply – ah for those days when the breathing-in of tobacco smoke was believed to be a certain defence against most varieties of germ. Ignorance was indeed bliss.

"Struggling," said I, smiling faintly.

"Hark here! Struggling!" exclaimed Big Bob, laughing to the others, and adding, to my surprise:

"We seen you doin' that side-path, kid; nice little cock-and-hen there, I'll bet."

That he had struck exactly the right price was impressive, and I was pleased with myself.

"What you up to?" I asked, in sympathy.

"Got an old *Mush* to *dik* (see) about a little tree job later, over by Netley Marsh, ain't it, Dinky?"

Dinky, small and dark and restless, smiled a reply:

"Sure it is, but he ain't no 'grunter' – proper old *rai* (gentleman)."

"Let's hope he's a good paymaster," observed Big Bob slightly pessimistically, adding, mournfully, "How about that Scotch cunt over Ferndown – tell him, Dinky."

"My mate you never seen nothin' like it," began Dinky, his black eyes shining with mixed emotions.

"We was over there calling an' Freddy took this job to cut the top off a couple of fir trees – must've gone fifty foot tall! Great *bori* (big) *kair* (house). Anyway, we just got the ladder by the first one when out comes the *rai* – turned from a lamb to a devil!

"'What the hell are you doing?' he shouts.

"'Just starting to top the trees, sir,' sez Bob.

"'What! I don't want no trees done!' he shouts, his face red as a fuckin' poppy. 'Clear off!' he goes, an' slammed the front door shut. Completely whipped on us!

"Well, we're starting to put the ladders back on the lorry when out he comes, all smiles.

"'Good morning,' he says. 'Just come to do the trees?'

"We sez yes an' he sez: 'Well, carry on,' an' goes back indoors. "Anyway we just got the ladders up when out he comes, hollerin' an' threatein' to send for the *gavvers*! (police) An' God strike me dead, just as we're packin' up for the second time he does no more than come out an' sez to carry on! I never seen nothin' like it in me life. Anyway we're up them fir trees like fuckin' ferrets an' had the tops off in five minutes. Bob went up to the door an' out he comes, all docile, an' pays up like a lamb! I tell you what, there's some funny old *foki* (people) about, *mush*. I don't want to meet many more like him, kid; too bad on your nerves!"

By this time their three full breakfasts had arrived, accompanied by a plate laden with white bread and butter.

"It's bad for your brains not to have a good breakfast, this is me second today," laughed Big Bob infectiously. His was an endearing personality, not to last overlong, alas. Indeed I attended his funeral when he was but forty nine, badly affected by heart problems exacerbated by his excessive weight.

Never violent unless provoked I recollect an incident one Saturday evening when, after baiting him because of his size six *Gaujo* youths attempted physically to overpower him. Although offered assistance by those of us in his company, he refused our offer.

"Nah!" he declared, "I can sort them little fuck-mothers out in two minutes."

What followed was an exhibition of controlled power – the six youths flying in all directions as he cast their struggling forms from him, deflected, landing awkwardly and painfully, their ferocity quelled. It was a pleasure to watch.

Having munched through their meals with the speed and tenacity of gannets they rose to leave. I too had finished eating, so we left together with an indifferent farewell from the proprietor.

"That man can't abear Travellers, ain't that right, Bob?" remarked Freddy, and he nodded in agreement.

"He's like his granny's old thing," added Dinky, spitting casually into an empty window box outside the café.

Strangely enough although not unaware of his thinly-veiled dislike Travellers seemed drawn to his establishment. From my experience it could not have been the quality of the food, or cooking, that appealed to them.

We went our different ways and I continued calling, but unfortunately my earlier luck deserted me and despite calling at a variety of dwellings, I seemed unable to secure a further job, either big or small. By one o'clock I found myself surrendering to the old adage: You can't make a good day out of a bad one. Accepting that principle I set off for home. At least I had earned ten pounds, which if viewed in the monetary values of today, was not a contemptible figure.

By the time I returned to the field Nelson and Liberty had also come back, Nelson's smart new Bedford parked beside his trailer and Liberty's slightly older, less powerful 25cwt Commer, painted in a rather dingy shade of maroon, was nearby.

They were both in good spirits, each of them having found employment in the field of tarmac laying on suburban drives. They had arranged the work for two separate days, thus allowing each to assist the other, and not necessitating the help of 'dossers' and so decrease their profits. Probably only brothers would adopt such a mutually advantageous stance.

'Dossers' have been part of the Travellers' lifestyle for many years, and right up to the present. In my experience they come in all shapes and sizes, and from no specific social strata. However, for the most part they seem to be social inadequates in one way or another. Many are drug addicts or alcoholics, sometimes being rescued from a life on the streets or gloomy hostels. There is no doubt that some, of a simple nature, have been taken advantage of by Travellers and very poorly financially rewarded – though, even then, surely preferable to living in cardboard boxes on the streets at the mercy of all. And then, of course, there are those who fit happily in the Traveller life, the lack of responsibility and frequent moving fitting well with their restless dispositions. Indeed, surprisingly large numbers have remained, working for the same Traveller families for decades, apparently content with their lot. Within such a mixture of humanity occasional calamities are bound to take place, but they are surprisingly rare in my experience.

The two brothers were undoubtedly impressed that, on my first attempt, I had found work even if on a lesser scale than their own.

"Little apples taste sweet, my dear old father always says," observed Nelson, his black eyes twinkling.

The idea of the hole cut in my van's roof still appealed to them greatly, causing them to peer through the back doors and stare up at the aperture in wonder.

To me, however, it was a sign of poverty and failure.

From that day I made it my aim to obtain a 30cwt lorry, even one of some age. The horse-for-courses princip0le must be applied.

For the rest of the week I stumbled on, taking several small jobs – footpaths, and even two or three driveways – the last of which was on a gradient of something in the nature of one-in-six. It looked quite attractive on completion, but I knew that the first heavy shower of rain would undoubtedly wash it down to the pavement below, luckily not contemplated by the householder, or if so then certainly not voiced.

It called to mind the experience of a Traveller friend of mine who completed the tarmac laying on a sloping drive, only to be told by the irate employer that he had wanted it finished in red! Taken aback by this turn of events my friend gave assurances that he could colour the tarmac to the requisite shade. It was, naturally, a promise made at random in an attempt to remedy a situation in which he could envisage his payment being halved – or worse. After some hours of scouring all kinds of shops and warehouses selling paints, distempers and the like, he was eventually persuaded to purchase a supposedly new, plastic infused, water-based solution, the congruence of which was guaranteed, its colour that of sundried tomatoes. Indeed, so impressed was the anxious shopper that he collected several drums – trusting that it could be applied via the nozzle of his tar sprayer.

Happily for my friend he found that the pliable mixture met with a sympathetic response from his tar sprayer and the whole surface was amended to a luscious crimson: a colouration greatly appreciated by the faintly eccentric house holder, who paid instantly for the service. Alas, however, that night a summer deluge brought disaster in its wake. To the consternation of the drive owner, and his neighbours, the water-based solution abandoned the tarmac, sending crimson rivulets gushing, like the blood of a slain elephant, down the adjoining pavement and roadway, gradually disappearing in the distance.

One could not help but feel that the likelihood of another 'knocker' in the locality achieving any sort of success was distinctly remote.

Before the above calamity I had myself called in the same area, one in which large detached houses sat amidst cultivated gardens, well-tended by their owners or their lackeys.

I called at one such house, hawking organic compost, when I espied two persons, a man and woman of early middle-age, both standing by a commodious looking fishpond, their eyes fixed upon it. Walking across the lawn in order to apprise them of my mission, I was taken by the sight of several large fish swimming lethargically in and out amongst the vast leaves of some kind of water lily.

"Good afternoon," I greeted them, with no great hopes. Upon close inspection they proved to belong to that class of person for whom 'class' was an aim in itself.

They looked wordlessly at me, the woman in a peach coloured cardigan over a floral dress of restrained colouration, whilst the man, clean shaven with short hair well brilliantined also in a cardigan, coupled with pale trousers.

A mischievous thought struck me, the result of which could fall either way.

"What lovely fish," I observed. "What are they?"

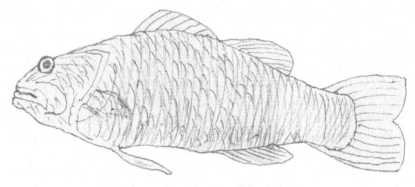

Specimen Fish

"That one is a silver orfe," replied the woman, pointing at a glistening monster on her left.

"What is that?" I enquired, pointing to another of different colour.

"Oh, that's a golden orfe," answered the man, eyeing me coldly.

At the moment a huge dark grey fish emerged from under the leaves.

"What is that one – a fuck orfe?" I said, endeavouring to lighten the moment.

It was some time before I could fully cast their reaction to my gentle witticism from my mind. Frozen, as though pole-axed, their expressions turned to scarce repressed fury.

"I'll pretend I didn't hear that – now kindly leave my property," he ordered.

I took that as a direct invitation to go, and obliged. It was not until I was outside on the road that I realised that the cause of my visit had not even been mentioned. However, I deemed it unwise to re-enter the garden and make it known to them. It seemed unlikely that a sale would have resulted.

Continuing over the next three weeks or so, all three of us managing to take jobs, sometimes from the wary and suspicious, other times from the pleasant and amiable, even from the downright simple – we were not too discriminating – until, eventually, the farmer received a visit from 'the Council' ordering him to remove us from his ground, it being 'unlicensed for the stationing of caravans' for anything in excess of the '28 days only in one year' rule concocted in order to disabuse landowners of the ludicrous idea that we were living in a free country without constraints on our mode of existence. The farmer was apologetic and indignant and resentful, as a ratepayer, of the action threatened against him. After a brief discussion between us, and working on the 'There's always another time' principle, we agreed to pull out by the weekend. Nelson and Liberty had an uncle who owned a tyre storage yard at a place called Bishops Waltham, no great distance away, and he had offered to let them stop there for a 'week or two'. With the generosity of their family they made it clear that we were welcome to join them if we wished.

But, I decided, it would be better to return to Fryern, sell the waggon, and try to find a 30cwt lorry instead of the Bedford van.

And so, with genuinely fond farewells we parted on the Sunday, Nelson and Liberty to the insalubriously closed in tyre yard, and us once more heading for the freedom of Fryern for, hopefully, more 'chops and changes' in our possessions.

Chapter 6

Out at 'Fortinbree'

We arrived back at Fryern in cheerful mood, the waggon still nestling beside the tall protective hedge. Sad and desolate though it appeared in its uninhabited state, we were pleased to see it – even though its disposal was imminent and inevitable.

Unbeknown to us then was the fact that this was to be our last stay within the agreeable confines of Fryern. Later that year was to mark the passing of the great artist and writer, the original *Romani Rai*, linguist and scholar, Augustus John. He died at home, in his early eighties, after a splendid life in which the drabness of self-denial played little part. His long-term 'wife' Dorelia was to follow a few years later. I have never visited the house since he left so I am uninformed as to its condition or occupants.

During that last stay I found myself paying more than a little attention to the town of Fordingbridge, known as 'Fortinbree' to the local Travellers.

In retrospect I find so many of the denizens of the town and its environment so fascinating, some eccentric, that I feel that they deserve immortalizing individually.

I first became aware of the existence of 'Smokey' in the main street of Fordingbridge on a sunny morning. Robust of stature, with black shoulder-length hair and walrus moustache, each earlobe burdened with a heavy ring, he was of some interest to the casual observer; the interest heightened, perhaps, by his garments – a multiplicity of checks and stripes, of strident colours and uneasy matching. Narrow moleskin trousers and heavy brown boots completed his outfit, most of his fingers enjoying the company of sturdy silver rings in a variety of heady designs. It was not the garb of the average man in the street.

We broke into conversation, each perhaps sensing the other's curiosity.

Addressing me in a voice still bearing echoes of the Black Country he was, I soon discovered, more than obsessed with the persona which he appeared to have cultivated enthusiastically for the benefit of his own ego. Whilst talking to me of himself he had about him, although a man of forty years or more, the enthusiasm that one might have expected in one half his years. Indeed, imagining me to be a good audience, his surging accounts of his life became unstoppable. To his credit, and in the manner of the true egocentric, he offered no questions to me about myself.

I was thus able to ascertain that he had been employed for some years as the 'Tent Master' of the late Billy Smart of circus fame. So enthused did he become that he requested that Beshlie and I might visit him in order that we could inspect his books of press-cuttings which, perhaps strangely, he seemed to think would be of interest to us.

He was then, he told me, employed in the management of a vast broiler-house, situated just out of the town, and owned by a youngish millionaire of dilettante tendencies. The last fact I found quite interesting, and having been given directions, I arranged our visit for the following evening at about seven o'clock.

Once home I told Beshlie of our evening engagement, and with whom it was. After receiving further details her faint enthusiasm disappeared altogether. She had never been a person for whom a social life has been a goal: rather has the avoidance of contact with strangers been her ambition.

Nevertheless, after a little coaxing, she agreed to accompany me on the unpromising visitation. Following the rather skimpy directions with which I had been provided, we eventually found ourselves alongside a poultry house of frightening proportions: truly a scar on the landscape. Permission for its presence could only have been approved by members of the Planning Authorities suffering severe visual impediment. From its immediate vicinity a noxious odour emanated, hanging heavily on the evening air.

"What a fucking awful place," observed Beshlie, as usual snatching the correct phrase for the moment.

Driving the Bedford cautiously along a track leading towards the rear of the monstrous building, we beheld a dismal and colourless little trailer-caravan lurking in the shadow of an outbuilding, a portable television aerial affixed to the guttering. An aged Trojan van (a rarity even in those times) stood nearby, dark grey and shabby.

Hearing our motor-engine Smokey emerged from the trailer, distinctly less gloriously attired than had been the case when I had met him in the town. This time he sported what might generously be termed the Casual Domestic Look; it comprised a long-sleeved woollen vest, baggy old navy blue serge trousers and carpet slippers. Even an Adonis would have found it well-nigh impossible to rise above such an array of unflattering garments.

Once ushered inside we were confronted by a very pallid, ravaged-looking woman of uncertain years, also wearing carpet slippers: the rest of her garments of no interest whatsoever. She was smoking a seemingly rather hostile cigarette, the agitations of which reduced her to intermittent bouts of faintly alarming heavy bronchial coughing.

Her accent, however, was quite musical, suggesting a South Devon origin – an unexpected bonus and a pleasant aural balm.

Introduced as Nance, but addressed as Mam by the boisterous Smokey, one was sympathetic towards her, although her role was difficult to fathom on so short an acquaintance. She appeared to be of benign temperament and, putting her knitting aside, immediately made tea for us in fetching floral-patterned mugs,  sweet and strong as was our taste. This was prior to our inspection of the press-cuttings, which we awaited with some trepidation. Not entirely groundless, we found, after being presented with page after page of photographs of Smokey posing, animatedly, in an astonishing variety of costumes, in checks, spots and stripes haphazardly mingled together for maximum eye-catching effect. All were culled from the pages of mainly provincial broadsheets, with a tiny proportion from more mainstream newspapers.

The captions were wildly inventive, some in would-be tabloid style, each reporter struggling to unearth an enticing fact to place before the public. Not, it transpired, an easy task when it was discovered that the entertainment value of the subject was almost entirely constrained to his own appearance.

After perusing an unending flow of such contrived images our spirits began to flag.

There was no doubt that Smokey was a colourful out-going personality of no clearly definable talents, but, alas, of no real intrinsic source of idolatry to anyone other than himself. For the onlooker, at least, there lay the seeds of disappointment.

We made a few more visits, sometimes enlivened by the programmes being offered by the little black-and-white television set. A novelty to us, not to be enjoyed until the distant future of 1965!

In the latter year I won such an aid to gracious living in a village fete raffle. It afforded us immense pleasure, gaining its power from the battery of our lorry by means of two powerful 'crocodile' clips. When viewing in the confines of the trailer of Smokey our programme selection was ruled by himself. Hence later, with our own set, we came to realise that there were more rewarding programmes than 'Bootsie and Snudge' or the abysmal 'Beverley Hillbillies,' both of which were the staple diet of entertainment appreciated by Smokey, and possibly the mournful Nance.

Upon the occasion of one of our last visits we found 'The Captain' under the amused audience of 'The Millionaire,' wrestling with the intricacies of the Trojan van's engine – ailments were afflicting it, I was informed, that threatened its consignment to the nearest car-breaker's yard.

"She've been a good old motor, any road – been round the clock twice," Smokey said proudly. Adding for greater effect: "And been up every steep hill in the country, pulling the old trailer. Billy Smart said he'd never seen nothing like it."

The Millionaire became convulsed with laughter at that point, to my surprise and the obvious chagrin of Smokey.

"Dear old Billy Smart," remarked The Millionaire to me. "He loved having the crack with The Captain – isn't that right, Smokey?"

Smokey avoided a reply, but surreptitiously rolled his eyes at me when The Millionaire's attention was diverted.

Theirs' seemed an uneasy alliance; their attitudes being that of jovial disdain, fairly well-hidden on the part of The Millionaire, whilst Smokey's was a mixture of resentment and envy.

My opinion of Smokey was to change for the worse, however, after meeting him one day in the street. The conversation, as always, was not allowed to veer from himself. To my astonishment he pulled from his pocket a West Country newspaper and drew my attention to an article recounting the tale of a man sentenced for assault. Further inspection revealed that the accused had entered into an angry exchange of words 'with a man who looked like Wild Bill Hickok' after a near-miss collision in their motor vehicles. Alarmed, he claimed, by the bizarre aspect of the other driver, who proved to be Smokey, and his supposedly threatening behaviour, he had struck out at random, landing a blow of some ferocity and blackening his opponent's eye. Here, however, the account took a turn for the worse. Far from taking the normal course of retaliating 'Wild Bill' had resorted to the despicable action of calling the police and, worse still, pressing charges!

I was so shocked on reading the cutting that I took my leave without delay.

In regards to being assaulted my mind turned to an incident that I suffered myself in Oxford. It was a sunny day in July, in late afternoon, when I was walking down St. Giles towards the city. At that period of time Oxford had become something of a magnet for alcoholics. The latter, from varied backgrounds, mostly broken-down by their addictions, would prowl about the streets, often two or three in numbers, accosting the timorous or unwary and demanding money as their due.

On the occasion I recall the approach of two such persons, one heavyset and wild-looking, the other small and dark with a staggering limp.

I instinctively knew that I would draw their attention, but did not foretell *my own* reactions.

Gathering around me they made their expected demands, leering and exhaling liquor-fumed breath upon me.

"You fucking bastards! Fuck off!" I heard myself exclaiming, to my own dismay. Better, and more advised, would it have been to have kept such remarks in check.

Leering benevolence turned to outraged fury from each.

"Ah, no one calls me a fucking bastard!" cried the smaller man, delivering a sharp blow to my ribs, whilst his companion aimed a huge fist to my face. The latter made contact with my mouth with the force of a pick-handle – two of my front teeth simultaneously bidding their roots farewell and landing on the pavement before me.

This two-handed approach and its dental consequences had left me unsteady and dazed, so I sat down.

At that moment, the two assailants having left the scene, a well-intentioned citizen emerged from a doorway, announcing:

"I saw what happened, I have called the police – they'll be here in a minute."

Indeed at that moment a 'jam-sandwich' car drew up and out stepped a uniformed constable and a female colleague.

I was still sitting on the pavement, sucking at the roots of my two snapped off upper front teeth.

"We know who did this," said the female constable brightly. "We just need a statement from you and we'll charge them."

They smiled expectantly.

"It was entirely my fault, I'm bringing no charges," I replied.

119

At this unwelcome reply they eyed me with cold disgust and, closing their notebooks, re-entered their car and drove away – offering me no assistance whatsoever.

Thus, in very low spirits, caused firstly by my stupidly aggressive reply to the alcoholics, and further by their unsurprising retort, I decided to walk to the nearest hospital for a tetanus injection. This was advised by a passer-by who offered to drive me to the 'A&E' department. However, upon being apprised of my intention not to press charges the suggestion of transportation was denied: their interest in my condition suddenly evaporated.

Upon reaching the hospital, after a walk of about a mile, I found the requisite department almost filled with obviously injured patients of varying ages and sexes. I was told that I might have to wait for an hour or two for attention.

Sitting down beside an infinitely respectable looking couple, in their thirties I judged, I was struck by the presence of a kind of tea-towel swathed around the head of the be-spectacled young woman.

Upon sympathetic questioning from myself as to the cause of her accident I was informed by her husband, in rather reedy tones, that a saucepan, dislodged by their cat from a shelf beneath which she was seated, had fallen upon her skull, damaging its surface. He then enquired of my facial injuries with some apparent sympathy. I explained my state to them both, during which explanation whey beamed at me, nodding the while.

We relapsed into silence, broken after some minutes by the man, leaning toward me confidentially to say:

"My wife and I are both committed Christians and are very impressed by your forgiveness of those men who attacked you."

Somewhat taken aback by this misjudgement of my character I was almost lost for words. Eventually, however, I allowed them to sink into their cocoon of naiveté: to have disabused them of their error would have been of no advantage to any of us.

After almost an hour and a half, with little decrease in the numbers awaiting treatment, I could wait no more. So with split lip- and throbbing tooth-roots I decided to take my chances and left.

The next day I found a dentist who was willing to remove the roots, which he did with dexterity and surprisingly little pain. My lip gradually healed of its own accord after a month or so. And I visited yet another dentist who successfully bridged the gap with two new teeth – one of gold! I was better than new! But best of all, my pride was intact. Not through me did another human being suffer imprisonment.

As always, life took an unexpected turn in regards to my Bedford van. Its unusual body-shaping had been a cause of attraction to Smokey, who upon the demise of his Trojan workhorse expressed a desire to become its new owner – a wish that I was more than willing to cultivate. A number of mechanical malfunctions were becoming a source of some concern to me: it was time for a new home. I explained my need for a lorry in order to further my gravel-laying pursuit, and conveyed my willingness to accept a 'reasonable' price for it.

It was thus, with no heaviness of heart, that I agreed a price with Smokey and concluded the deal in a remarkably short space of time. A week or so later I encountered him and he ruefully related the number of faults that he had discovered within the ill-served vehicle.

A communication with Nelson uncovered the fact that one of his cousins, bearing the unfortunate nickname of Pig's Head, had just 'chopped-in' his old A-type Bedford lorry for a new one. Six years old, high in mileage, but with tipping gear as an added bonus, it sounded just what I needed – my expectations not being too high.

It was to be found at a Bedford Dealership near Southampton, and I resolved yet again to engage the services of Gilly to drive me over to view it.

He arrived promptly the next morning and we were soon on the road towards Southampton. Not a health-inducing journey, Gilly having filled the little van the previous day with half a ton of chicken manure. The latter having left a residue of ammonia-tainted ordure, the fumes of which hung heavily within the confines of the Morris van, causing me to cough and grunt incessantly. Gilly, as ever, found refuge in his Capstone Full Strength cigarettes, for which ordure posed little competition.

"Cah, you've had some deals, lately, mate," he remarked approvingly.

"Got to do something to stop going broke," I smiled.

"Bloody hell! There'll be hairs growing on a diamond 'fore that," he replied, grinning gummily at me, his face engagingly patterned in a mixture of sweat and dirt. The latter, he assured me, being proof against both cold and germs. According to such reckoning this must surely have made him the warmest and healthiest inhabitant of the New Forest, I mused.

The Main Dealer proved rather different to my previous experiences within the motoring world. Fronted by an expansive display of brand new Vauxhall and Bedford models, the Bedford being Commercials, at the forefront, the rear being the place wherein lurked the 'pre-owned' motors of varying condition.

121

Within that area it was easy to discern the 30cwt Bedford lorry, the cause of my visit. At close quarters its Travellery qualities were instantly recognizable to the initiated. Painted in two tones of bright blue, with additional expanses of staring chrome upon the bumpers, radiator grille, and side mirrors, it was not the aspect cultivated by the average practical artisan. It instantly appealed to me with such extras: it even boasted a sturdy 'step' drawbar of the design favoured by Travellers when towing heavy trailer-caravans.

It was priced at a hundred and twenty pounds with 'One Owner' as an added attraction.

A portly, oily-haired salesman in a rumpled suit and shining black shoes, sidled up to us. His attitude was guarded, not too enthusiastic: I wondered if he detected a whiff of the malodorous ordure which I fancied still lingered about our persons.

"Are you commercials?" I enquired, not wishing him to wander in the maze of error concerning the type of vehicle that we sought.

"I am," he said. "What do you want – a lorry or a van?"

"This is what I've come to see," I replied, pointing to the blue lorry.

"Oh, a nice clean motor for its year," he began, warming to the subject. "It belonged to one of our nomadic brethren, he had it from new and he's looked after it. For the year you would be lucky to find one as clean."

His spiel completed he looked for a reaction.

With slight hesitation he agreed to a test drive, insisting on affixing trade-plates before embarking on such a course.

There was none of the fun or exhilaration that I had felt in my dealings with Travellers, and the Hillyer brothers, so I felt a little dispirited.

The test seemed, at least ostensibly, to prove that the lorry was still in reasonable condition. Any secret faults remained secret.

After the test drive the Main Dealer and I returned to his office, wherein Gilly had remained, comfortable in his own aura of the medley of ordure and full-strength Capstone, the pungency of which was fumigation of a high calibre, causing both the Main Dealer and myself to relapse into bouts of coughing.

"How was she?" he enquired solicitously.

"Seems okay," I replied cautiously.

The Main Dealer looked on noncommittally. Humour, I concluded, was not part of the exercise.

Indeed, after rather lacklustre exchanges between us we finally agreed on the sum of one hundred pounds cash for the transaction. In those days a brand new 30 cwt Bedford was in the region of six to seven hundred pounds only. In retrospect a paltry sum, yet at the time it caused one's financial resources to quail.

To the slight surprise of the Main Dealer, after telephoning my insurance company and asking for 'Third Party' Cover I drove the lorry homewards. It had two days' worth of Tax left on the disc, so I was surprisingly legal. Indeed, I recollect that from the late 'fifties until the end of the 'seventies the taxing of their vehicles was not viewed with enthusiasm by many itinerant Travellers – myself included. The maxim: "She runs as well without it" was the commonest rejoinder when questioned by an over-zealous policeman. The latter generally accepted the situation with an admiral degree of resignation, wisely deciding that the effort involved in tracing the culprits outweighed the result.

The little lorry, although something of an oil-burner, and equipped with temperamental brakes, as well as a defective exhaust, was nonetheless vastly superior to our previous Bedford van.

There was a faintly raffish air about it, its appearance evoking salutations from any other Travellery lorry or van we encountered. In a sense we became part of a secret road-users' club – one with which I have endeavoured to retain membership to this day, more subtle though the congress has become.

It remained in our ownership for three years, becoming the vehicle longest-held in our possession before or since.

Two or three days later, whilst waiting for Beshlie who was purchasing food supplies from the gay grocers, two identical Jaguar saloons drew up behind me. The two cars, sporting the license plates of UY1 and UY2, disgorged the figures of both Smokey and his employer The Millionaire. The latter, immaculate in blue-and-white striped shirt, French blue silk-shot slacks, and expensive suede loafers, hurried towards me, manner frenetic, hand outstretched.

"We've just been to collect Up Yours One from the garage, after its service. Up Yours Two next week, eh Captain? We've been having the crack – the Captain likes the crack, don't you?"

'The Captain' gave no indication of enjoyment, other than smiling faintly at passers-by who gazed in wonder at his curious garb and hirsute appearance. The last, of course, with the coming of the 'sixties and the accompanying revolutions in hair-styles and dress, was to lose its bizarre aspect: the amazement would lessen. Such deprivation must surely have dented his ego.

The Woosterish manner cultivated by The Millionaire was a little trying but not too tedious. How could anyone be tedious who had the effrontery to own *two* Jaguars and impose such number-plates upon them?

Just outside of Fordingbridge, beside a place with the alluring name of Godshill, there was a privately-owned enclosure of woodland and field, with the even more fanciful name of Sandy Balls! To the stranger, expecting to find perchance, the residence of an exiled Scot with arenaceous testes, his surprise must have been inordinate upon discovering it to be a form of holiday retreat equipped for its denizens with multifarious accommodation, ranging from chalets and sheds, to a few elderly vintage caravans, and an unusual number of differing old wooden waggons, some of showmen origin and others Romani; mostly long since devoid of any roadworthiness and some propped up by vertically arranged railway sleepers. All were painted in startling colours and their aura was incredibly pleasing beneath the trees.

Upon closer investigation I discovered it to be a veritable nest of eccentrics, of the folksy and arty-crafty persuasion and appearance, no longer found in any numbers, living in apparently festive community: I found it fascinating though not enviable.

Alas, I was not to know it but tragedy was to strike one of their would-be neighbours.

Beshlie and I were seated outside our trailer on a sunny evening at Fryern when we were aware of a solitary figure approaching us from the gate. Closer proximity revealed him to be a man of late middle-age of extraordinarily astounding height, well over six and a half feet, his features all but obliterated by cascading white hair and a 'ram in a thicket' beard of prophet-like dimensions – fully eighteen inches in length, spreading across his chest. Clad in a seaman's navy jersey, putty-coloured corduroy trousers, with bare feet in open sandals, he was indeed riveting. He peered benignly at us through bright blue eyes.

"Hello" he introduced himself, "I'm William Monk. I was sent here by someone who says you have a gypsy caravan for sale. Is that correct?"

Having discovered the identity of the person who sent him, a 'dealing man' from near Salisbury, we were pleased to confirm that it was the case.

Seated beside the fire, the evening sunlight playing brightly upon his hair and beard, his air of benevolent mysticism became more than a little pronounced. He gave every indication of being the dream-customer for our waggon.

"That's the waggon," I explained, pointing along the hedgerow.

"It looks to be what I am seeking," he replied, his voice deep yet modulated, controlled, hinting at theatrical pretensions. He seemed to be an extraordinarily pleasant person, with an impact of charisma.

After a little conversation he divulged that his career had, in fact, been that of an actor, both in films and on the stage.

"The most lowly art-form, I fear," he concluded, smiling at us.

Having inspected the waggon, and being especially charmed by its little old-fashioned 'Queenie' cast-iron fuel burning stove, it was made clear to us that, if he bought the waggon, he would wish to find a spot in sympathetic surroundings where he could live. 'Sandy Balls' instantly sprang to mind and, with repressed mirth, we apprised him of its situation and details of the owner – a retired medical man of vegan tendencies.

Thus, subject to his approval of the New Forest caravanserai, we agreed upon a price, and I undertook to find someone who would transport the waggon to its destination.

As he was anxious to complete the deal quickly in order to move-in, it was arranged for him to telephone Fryern at one o'clock the next day. The telephonic communication readily agreed by Dorelia, whose amiability and generosity towards us never faltered.

The next morning passed slowly as we awaited, with some misgivings, the telephone call from the actor. However, I was not kept long at Fryern, the call coming through at the appointed hour. The dulcet tones of William Monk flowed steadily and distinctly across the air waves, with the more than welcome news that 'Sandy Balls' exactly measured up to his requirements. All that remained was for me to arrange the transportation of the waggon and collect the money at the same time. Not far from Ringwood was a settled-down Traveller of my acquaintance known as Black Sid. Living with his wife, in a small wooden bungalow on their own land, he was of an independent turn of mind, though generally tractable in the face of financial inducement. He was officially a Scrap Merchant, but was elastic in his occupations. First and foremost, however, was the fact that he owned a car-transporter lorry upon which the waggon would easily fit. On our last meeting he had given me his business card, a new venture for him, and it contained his telephone number.

Upon ringing the number I was greeted by Sid himself, gruff of voice and aggressive in manner.

"Hullo – WHO'S THAT?" It was not the most endearing tone. However, upon learning who was calling he immediately became more affable, assuring me that he could perform the task that very evening. Upon my questioning him about the cost he dismissed it airily.

"Well, it ain't too far, *mush*. If you're paying I won't hurt you – just gimme a nice drink, we shan't fall out over that, kid."

There was not much more to be said, and the arrangement was sealed. Both Beshlie and myself were more than delighted at the way in which matters were proceeding. Now all we had to do was await the arrival of Black Sid, with whom I had not crossed paths for almost a year.

True to his word he appeared at the gate soon after five o'clock, sitting in the cab of his lengthy car-transporter – the latter displaying Trade Plates for the occasion.

Although rumoured to be a man of wealth Black Sid's appearance rather belied the fact. Deeply swarthy of complexion, his features gaunt and heavily lined, with glittering dark eyes he carried a sinister look. On his head perched a battered black trilby, his figure encased in a dank-looking boiler-suit, set off by aged yellow jodhpur boots. He was tall and running to fat around his middle and erratic of movement. Beside him sat a youth of about sixteen, with the kind of Romani face rarely encountered today – his Indian ancestry being undeniable. Black Sid addressed him a Paki Henry, which appeared to cause him neither embarrassment nor resentment, and it was used without malice.

"Got me right-hand man here to help," observed Black Sid, poking Paki Henry in the ribs.

Having been shown the waggon Black Sid and his assistant lost no time in loading it on to the transporter, and I joined them in the cab to give them directions to our destination.

Being without the benefit of literacy Black Sid was unable to notice the eccentricity of the 'Sandy Balls' signpost at the entrance but merely expressed relief that the gateway was wide enough to negotiate without fear of mishap.

Once inside we were immediately intercepted by the looming figure of William Monk who pointed to the location he had chosen, between two of the older Romani Waggons, each one crumbling on its chassis yet with decorously painted bodies in adventurously bold colours.

"*Dordi!*" exclaimed Black Sid on catching sight of William Monk.

"He's like the Dear Blessed Lord hisself, on my life – eh Henry?"

Paki Henry's eyes widened in surprise but he remained non-committal.

The sight of the jovial-looking William Monk was a relief to me. I perceived a rather thick-set woman, standing beside him, with some astonishment. Bespectacled and rosy-cheeked, with unusually thick grey hair, worn in a single plait that reached to her waist; her apparel was an exciting combination of colour-enhanced tweed and multi-textured accoutrements apparently knitted in string of varying hues. Her feet, like those of William Monk, enjoyed the freedom of open-work sandals. A mass of necklaces and beads, together with numerous silver rings on most of her fingers all provided her with an agreeably bohemian aspect, I thought.

Black Sid and Paki Henry completed the task of unloading the waggon, and placing it in exactly the position that was directed.

Looking in vain for any signs of the buyer's possessions I eventually realised that he had stored them in the waggon belonging to the lady.

It was an old showman's waggon from the Victorian era, painted in a mix of mauves and purples, but in an advanced state of decay. Its owner, with the surprisingly mundane name of Cath, had apparently lived in it for eight years. Beside its towering bodywork our waggon seemed miniscule, and scarcely roomy enough for the bulk of William Monk. He did, however, seem delighted by it – pressing an envelope into my hand, assuring me that it contained the requisite sum upon which we had agreed. Thanking him I pushed the envelope into my coat pocket, buttoning-down the flap. There was, I knew, no need to insult him by counting it out in front of him. There are, in life, times when one must back one's own judgement – and this was one of them.

Black Sid, sensing something of a 'grunter' in the person of William Monk, stood by expectantly. Taking his cue the actor responded cheerily, thrusting a five pound note into the grubby hand of Sid, merely smiling at Paki Henry – whose eyes rolled in resignation.

The whole operation had taken less than an hour, and I was soon deposited outside Fryern, and presented Black Side with 'a nice drink.' I strode over to the trailer, gazing nostalgically at the empty space where our last waggon had rested.

I was advised by a local ancient Traveller-woman against making any visits to 'Sandy Balls,' warning me against the tenants, hinting darkly at their maledictory powers, disguised behind their benevolent folksy display

"They'm bad-minded 'omans an' men," she declared to me. Adding: "They looks up to the *Beng* (Devil) hisself."

After several visits I discovered that some of the little group were Budhists, others Pagan or Pacifists. Their union with the Devil was not apparent, to the untrained eye.

Amongst their number was an artist named Aylwyn Finch, with whom I struck up a limited friendship. To me his most admirable characteristic was the fact that he earned a precarious living by calling door to door in suburbia, offering his service as a child portrait-painter. In fact, his pictures were executed in pastel, with enough skill to enrapture the mothers of his infant subjects. He generally proceeded on his rounds by bicycle or, if traversing longer distances, by bus. His manner was gentle, his features long and white, with hair of a suitably artistic length.

He resided in a small shed, one of several at 'Sandy Balls', no more twelve feet by six feet. Its interior was very sparse, with none of the chintzy and cluttered qualities of such dwellings when owned by Travellers. In fairness to him I should mention that he was dedicated to the pursuance of the once sought-after Simple Life. Existing entirely on uncooked food, with a preponderance of nuts, dried fruit and lentils, with occasional luxuries of fruit and vegetables, he was a vegan, eschewing all meats and dairy produce. Alas, compared to either Black Sid or Paki Henry, the figure that he presented to the world was closer to Mahatma Gandhi than Mr Universe. Thus, with his poor physique and inadequate clothing one felt that he could be blown from this world by the tiniest of disasters.

The only person with whom he appeared to have any bonding at all was a strange German ex-prisoner of war – for whom Sandy Balls provided uncritical sanctuary. Known merely as Helmut this peculiar Teuton lived in fear of rain, whether heavy or fine. To protect himself from its imagined ravages he adopted a very personal form of dress consisting of transparent plastic sheeting. Whatever the weather, summer or winter, he was never without its protective covering, even his hat was so equipped. In the hottest days of summer he refused to slough off the odious fabric. However, socialising with scarce a soul, save Aylwyn Finch, he posed no nuisance to anyone, and remained unmolested during his occasional safaris to Fordingbridge. On two occasions I tried to engage him in conversation whilst he was pushing his shopping-laden bicycle along the main street of Fordingbridge, but each attempt was met with guttural mutterings and a steeling glare: hardly the best example of post-war Germany's attempts at reconciliation.

It was not an entirely one-sided reaction.

A retired London rag-and-bone man and his withering old wife, Joe and Daise, with whom I had an amiable alliance, were both furious at the German's effrontery in setting up home in the locality of their adoption.

"We was bombed-out by them Jerries," grumbled Joe – lost every bloody thing we had, mate. Ain't that right, Daise?"

Daise nodded in agreement, spitting into the gutter.

"Bloody bastards – they got no rights to be here. Pack 'em off home, I say," continued Daise, her pallid face contorted with malice.

Had I been in their place I had no doubt that I would have felt the same.

Of the folksy and bohemian residents at Sandy Balls perhaps the most interesting was a figure of both physical and intellectual stature called Professor Donald Henham. Although over six feet in height, with the features of the film star of the 'thirties and 'forties named Robert Donat, he managed to exist, alone, in a tiny touring caravan of dimensions scarce exceeding six feet by ten feet. Within this tiny cell the professor earned his living by means of translations from numerous languages, for both business and private employers. Amongst the languages demanding his services were: Icelandic, Finnish, Danish, Swedish and Bulgarian! That one man could accommodate such linguistic gymnastics was beyond my comprehension – I was utterly staggered. Although I did in fact become quite friendly with him my innate inferiority complex limited my conversation in a manner hitherto quite unfamiliar to me.

He did not fit in with the folksy group, and was not drawn to the German, hence he lived a solitary existence. Confining his mornings to translations, his afternoons spent in long exploratory walks in the New Forest and its environs, the simplicity of his life-style was entirely of his own making and, in many ways more successful than that of Aylwyn Finch.

It was strange to find such a varied band of 'seekers' conglomerated in so small a space.

It was whilst still at Fryern that I encountered, by chance, a veterinary herbalist and author with the striking name of Juliette de Bairacli-Levy. She was at the time living in a small rented cottage called Abbots Well, not far from the idyllically named hamlet of Blissford, on the edge of the New Forest.

It was a 'forester,' bred and born in the New Forest, named Johnny Snow who told me of her existence and of his brushes with her.

"She's a funny little woman s'know," he said. "You sometimes sees her swimmin' in they brooks, up over where she'm to," he continued. "Otherwise she'm up be the cottage behind the fence lyin' naked in the sun," he informed me, waiting for the effect of his statement. Further information revealed that she was accompanied by the presence of her small son, fathered by a Spaniard I was told.

"She'm that sunburned she'm like a little black beetle," said Johnny, warming to his subject. "She writes they books," he concluded, which I found quite interesting.

I managed to engineer a meeting with the author, but like so many contrived visitations it was not a great success. It was obvious from the start that we were on different planes – neither superior, just different.

She was indeed a nut-brown little person of early middle-age, crowned by dense black corkscrew-curled hair, which she assured me had always grown straight until she contracted Typhus whilst in Spain! Despite losing all her hair and narrowly escaping death she finally recovered. Her hair returned, to her astonishment, in its present condition.

Living on herbs and fruit and vegetables, drinking only spring water, was the key to a long and healthy life she informed me. I had to confess that, rare in my experience of such devotees, she did truly emanate good health.

I did not meet her again, but was told, a few years later by Johhny Snow, that she had left the quietude of the New Forest for the hustle of New York.

The last information was imparted to me on a wholly unexpected meeting with Johnny Snow in the little town of Builth Wells where the annual Royal Welsh Show was being held. In an attempt to enlarge his geographical scope from the enclosure of his native New Forest, he had brought some ponies from there to the Royal Show, hoping to turn a profit. Unsurprised by his news of the herbalists's exit for foreign parts, I was not prepared for his next disclosure.

It concerned the demise of the faintly disenchanted-looking William Monk. Apparently, although fitting in well with his exotic neighbours, he was beset by inner demons, for no confessed reason. He was discovered one morning within our old waggon, by the worthy Cath, lying stiff and dead on the bed. He had, I was told, consumed a toxic drink of his own concoction – its contents guaranteed to execute the mission, even though its painfulness was acute.

He had written a note requesting that he should be cremated, which was addressed to Cath, to whom he left the waggon and his few possessions. Strangely enough I was unexpectedly distressed by the news, wishing that I had devoted more time to his cultivation before the terrible act of self-destruction heralded his final curtain.

In retrospect one could not but imagine him to have been one of the many talented persons who never found fulfilment in either their private lives nor in the profession of their choice. The mysticism of Good Luck seemingly rarely, if ever, their companion.

Sometime later, on a winter's morning in Fordingbridge, I was accosted by the dishevelled figure of Nance, paler than usual, water-eyed in the cold air.

"Smokey've been electrocuted," she announced without preamble. "He was in the chicken-shed and he touched the overhead cable – looked like killing him. He won't get out of bed, and the doctor sez he can't do nothing for him."

I expressed my sympathy and promised to visit him that evening.

When I arrived, before dark, the curtains were drawn in the trailer and upon my knocking the dazed-looking figure of Nance opened the door, the habitual cigarette clamped in one side of her mouth.

Upon entering I was a little surprised to see the patient, whom I had presumed to be at death's door, sitting-up, not recumbent as I had imagined, chuckling heartily at an episode of 'Bootsie and Snudge' on his little black-and-white television.

His features altered, however, on catching sight of me, assuming a mournful expression of deepest gloom.

Upon being asked how he felt he replied:

"It's the brain that's been hit – badly damaged I think. I was thrown ten feet down onto concrete, and it's a wonder I wasn't killed stone-dead by all them volts."

Nance and I stared at him, each digesting the significance of his words.

Cynical as ever I was forced to doubt the veracity of his diagnosis of his true condition. Would one indeed *realise* if one's actual brain was thrown asunder?

This was, of course, long before the age of Health and Safety, crash helmets, safety belts or other accoutrements of everyday life. The idea of suing an employer was not commonly acted upon. The Millionaire, however, must have sensed that something was expected of him. Within a short space of time he had equipped Smokey with a brand-new Austin pick-up and a brand new touring trailer caravan of high quality and elegant design. The possession of those two items appeared to have magical curative effects on the victim of electrocution: his brain recovered its egocentric vigour, his shambling gait returned to normality. It was all very spiritually uplifting.

I was to meet Smokey a few times in the ongoing weeks. It was faintly dispiriting to note that he had taken pains to personalize his blue Austin pick-up by means of the application of a number of floral transfers, in the shape of roses and carnations, about its cab and bodywork – an act liable to cause feelings of disorientation in the mind of the average onlooker. This was furthered by the addition of a brass plate just above the windscreen with the legend 'The Wandering Outcast' inscribed upon it.

His pride in the vehicle was undeniable, though strangely enough he declined to mention how this sudden change in his fortune had come about. As ever it was the effect that was foremost in his mind.

My last sighting of this outlandish person was in Cornwall one summer. It was quite near to St Ives and we and two other Traveller families and their trailers were slowed down by road repairs. My astonishment knew no bounds when, amongst the gang of navvies wielding picks and shovels, we perceived the figure of Smokey so engaged.

Slowly passing these toilers, I was merely able to shout a greeting to the erstwhile Tent Master, who appeared as surprised as ourselves.

In its coincidence and its finality there was, I felt, an almost Dickensian quality.

After Augustus died there was little or nothing to draw us back to Fordingbridge – a town filled with memories, both joyful and sad for me.

Whether or not 'Sandy Balls' still exists I know not. Though if it does I cannot imagine it being inhabited by the variety of persons I found there at the end of the nineteen fifties. Their likes have long since disappeared I strongly suspect. As too must the small numbers of Romani dwellings then within the area. I recollect one such, a collection of shacks in extreme dilapidation, mainly of corrugate iron and old canvas sheeting, known locally as 'Tin Town.' Within those earth floored habitations, whole families lived and bred under conditions that would bring about hysteria in the minds of the social workers of today. Their fate was to be denied, by the authorities, the right to roam the New Forest freely in their traditional way of life. Undoubtedly it was racism in its finest hour, achieving gradually its aim of obliteration. As always the poorer and most vulnerable were the greatest sufferers.

It was at 'Tin Town' that I had most connection with Bob and Queenie who, with their numerous very Romani-looking *Chavies* (children), had existed there for most of their married life, happy despite the privations. Electricity and 'sanitation' were unknown to them; and water was carried from a nearby spring. Several other families were their neighbours, some quite aged and worn-out, all inhabiting shacks of a strangely similar construction and appearance. The Local Authority, naturally, was not happy with such conditions – despite the fact that they were responsible for them! Their ambition, sadly eventually achieved, was to prepare such people for the glories of council-house tenancies. However, deeming such gypsy-people as too inferior for such immediate luxury, they placed many families in groups of old ex-army huts, dotted about the surroundings of the New Forest. It was decided by the councils that the experience of hut living, with electricity and running water, would prepare the people for the greater glory that lay ahead of them. As always, the suburban mentality was in charge.

I recall many visits to Bob and Queenie's humble earth-floored home, enjoying simple meals of meat pudding or fried bacon and bread and strong sweet tea: their hospitality was intense and generous.

Of the three or four such groups within a few miles of Fordingbridge, almost all were related; similar in feature, their homes all replicas of each other's in every detail.

Alas, it was not many years ahead before their fate was sealed and they were gradually almost all 'rehoused' – to be absorbed into the world of the low paid *Gaujo* (non-Traveller). For them the Romani Life had vanished forever, as so many of them degenerated into a kind of half-world – neither Travellers nor *Gaujo,* which for them was a confusing state to be in.

It is a situation in which many European Romanies find themselves since the old Romani Life was destroyed by the Nazis during World War II, and by other dictatorial regimes since.

Indeed even the most superficial study of the history of Romanies since they first arrived in Europe is a dismal catalogue of repression and prejudice; Britain by no means low on the list of offenders.

To be viewed as unwelcome lodgers in whatever country they have adopted would seem to be the fate of all too many Romanies.... and Jewish people too.

Chapter 7

Onward and Upwards

Restlessness, coupled with our sadness at the passing of Augustus John, decided us in our leaving Fordingbridge. Our departure was further encouraged when, 'calling' around Southampton, I passed by a well-used unofficial stopping place much frequented by Travellers. Situated on wasteland near to the docks it comprised no pleasing aspect. Rubbish-strewn, mostly by the local house dwellers who were fully aware that the Travellers would be blamed, it was no joyful site to behold. The nearest building was a vast baked beans factory of international repute; behind which there was a water-tap that was surreptitiously enjoyed by us all. It was the only amenity offered to those who chose to pull-on to the barren ground.

On this occasion just three trailers were in evidence. Two Eccles 'Travellers' and a large Berkeley were all grouped together in the way of related families. Two A-type Bedford lorries, like our own, stood by the trailers – a third vehicle still 'out.' They were obviously middle-of-the-road in their status, the kind of Travellers taking 'French Leave' and catching a few days wherever they could. It was a way of life that I still found attractive despite its persecution by over-zealous police or council officials. There was still about it an indefinable sense of freedom and excitement.

As I drew in from the road I recognized the turnouts as belonging to Joe, Joe-boy (his son) and Little Joe (the son of Joe-boy). Beshlie and I had been in their company many times.

Before I was close, the door of the Berkely trailer opened and Old Joe emerged. Aged around sixty, his swarthy and pitted features were unquestionably Romani. He wore an immaculate dark suit, collar and tie and polished shoes somewhat at odds with his face. It was, of course, his respectable apparel and polite conversation that enabled him to excel in the harrowing task of persuading suspicious householders to employ him in the re-surfacing of their drives or footpaths. He did, in fact, in defiance of the often slipshod methods of some Travellers, invariably produce results of unfailing skill. For him the 'squeals' of indignant house-owners was virtually unknown.

Although he and his wife Eileen had five other sons, all travelling, only their eldest, Joe-boy was with them just then – accompanied by their grandson Little Joe who was but recently married to his distantly related bride of but sixteen years old.

"Hello, my old kid," he greeted me, in a husky voice with a faint Welsh inflection. "Where's you stopping?" he enquired.

I told him of my plans to move immediately, at which he nodded.

"We're shifting tomorrow, he told me. "We're going down to South Wales for a few weeks – why don't you come with us?"

My spirits lifted at the thought, only to be dampened slightly when told that their son-in-law Bloodless Bob, who was estranged from their daughter, intended to make the journey too, in the forlorn hope of winning back his wife Letty. The latter feat could be sensibly viewed as unlikely to be achieved. After five children, some beatings, and innumerable quarrels, it would not have been advisable and, in fact, never eventuated, to the relief of all.

Wolf-like, cruel and hard, Bloodless Bob feared nobody apart from Old Joe's second son, Benjie, who had once served him so harshly that he almost bled to death before being given a transfusion which saved his life – hence his nickname. In that business the only admirable fact was that he did not have Benjie charged with assault. Rather did he assert to the disbelieving constabulary that his injuries had been the result of slipping down onto broken glass. However, Benjie and he retained complete silence toward each other, indeed, never conversing again in their lives. Good sound reasoning say I!

At that moment the attention of Joe and myself was distracted by the approach of an old Bedford van, pulling an even older little trailer towards us.

"Here come me son-in-law," said Joe, gazing contemptuously at the shabby turnout, now level with us. Upon closer proximity the state of both van and trailer was worse than it appeared in the distance. The van was an aged 1938, 30cwt model, dented and rusted in equal measure, its radiator steaming ominously. The little trailer, once the pride of a holiday maker no doubt, was bulging at the seams, scuffed down one side, and with most of the windows broken or missing.

Bloodless Bob jumped down from the cab, accompanied by a lurcher dog in mangy condition.

"How's things, Bob?" asked Joe, without enthusiasm.

"Been better, Uncle Joe," replied Bob, pulling down the brim of his hat and staring at me with no friendliness of expression.

I nodded at him, and he nodded back.

"You off to South Wales, I heard, Uncle Joe?" he remarked, a faint sneer playing permanently about his mouth.

"Yeah, goin' tomorrow," replied Joe distantly.

"Mind if I come with you, Uncle Joe? Only I wants to try to git my Letty back if I can," Bob informed us.

"Well, the roads is free, I can't stop you," said Joe, adding: "But as to my gal, well it's up to her. You've served her so bad – but I ain't gonna tell her what to do – she's a grown woman."

Undercurrents flowed in the conversation, apparent even to me.

I had not seen Bloodless Bob for a while, but he had in no way improved from the memories that I had of him. He was, without doubt, a dangerous man – and even more so since the disgrace of his wife leaving him, despite it being entirely his own fault.

Unbeknown to me, however, things were about to take a turn for the better.

When we arrived the next morning we were surprised to see that another trailer had joined them, a mid-sized Carlight, the Rolls Royce of trailers, pulled by a smart twin-wheeled Bedford lorry, painted in chocolate and cream. I recognised it as belonging to Joe's son Benjie, the one who had hospitalised Bob some time previously. Benjie and I were quite close friends and I knew that fact would protect me from any malicious attack, Bob's fear of Benjie being too great. With that in mind we pulled next to Benjie and his wife Marie, intending to follow close behind them on the unknown journey to South Wales.

It was around 11 o'clock in the morning and almost everyone was 'packed-down' and ready to be off. The weather was cool but without any apparent danger of rain.

Joe, as the Patriarch, led the way, followed by Young Joe, Little Joe, Benjie, ourselves, and Bloodless Bob last.

Hurtling along the roads as part of a convoy has always been a cause of excitement and pride to me, even if coupled with the complications of people running out of diesel or taking the wrong route! – the last never more alarming, perhaps, than an occasion near Bath when we were in a line of seven trailers, being led by a man of rather advanced years who, in a fit of disorientation, guided us all the wrong way around a busy roundabout, to the indignation, mystification, and fury of more conventional road-users! However, only time would tell whether or not a similar mishap might occur during our trip to South Wales. There was no denying that it was well within the bounds of possibility.

Our departure was not marked by any ceremony. Three or four ragged meths drinkers, existing in sub-standard bender tents, fashioned from any old carpet or canvas to hand, gazed at us from a distance across the ground; we did not mix socially.

Old Joe was never one to dawdle when on the move, maintaining a more or less steady forty to fifty miles per hour. A speed which none of us but Bloodless Bob found anything of a challenge. The powerful six cylinder petrol engines of our Bedfords were stout-hearted and reliable despite a degree of neglect by their owners. Indeed, during the three years that we kept the lorry that had been the proud possession of Pig's Head we were only once struck by misfortune.

We were in Cambridgeshire, on the road with three other trailers, when the clutch completely abandoned its function. Thus, complete with trailer and all our worldly possessions, we were immobilised on a desolate fenland roadside. Luckily, and without hesitation, one of the Travellers, who was familiar with the area, generously returned from our intended stopping-places with his lorry, pulled us there, and then towed my lorry to a Bedford agent some miles away. The agent was good-hearted and helpful, treating the matter as an emergency. Thus, setting to work on replacing the clutch without delay it was ready to drive away within a few hours. A payment of £13 was all that was required: but it was not a happy introduction to Cambridgeshire for us.

We proceeded steadily 'down country' until, by-passing Gloucester, we pulled onto a wide green verge beside a main road, deciding to stop there for the night. Beshlie, who had never enjoyed long journeys, welcomed the respite. Personally, I would have preferred the purer air of Wales.

After cooking ourselves a meal on outside fires the men decided on driving to a nearby roadhouse for a drink: for Old Joe and his sons it was an addiction, on seven nights a week.

All their wives were expected to provide them with a hot meal upon their return each night at about eleven o'clock.

"I likes a bit of sheep's paunch," declared Old Joe, adding roguishly: "Makes you fuck like a ferret!"

Unwilling to taste such a dish I was unable to vouch for the veracity of the assertion.

One could not help but feel slightly apprehensive as to the future of the sixteen years old bride of Little Joe upon marrying into a family of such alcoholic dedication. Despite this slight flaw, however, I found both Old Joe and his sons the best of company, all filled with a zest for their way of life, and a commendable sense of adventure and pride. It

137

was for such reasons that I allowed myself to be drawn into their company.

As most of Old Joe's sons and daughters seemed to breed an absolute minimum of five children apiece, and several eight and more, their contribution towards the continuation of the Romani people could only be applauded!

As Old Joe, his sons and grandson, all attired themselves in the Romani fashions of the time their effect upon the regular customers in the roadhouse was disturbing. The incongruity of the country gentleman check hats, Traveller-style yoke-backed and many pocketed tailor-made suits, coupled with yellow jodhpur boots, jarred within that setting. Although fully aware of the attention our appearance provoked we chose to ignore it, apart from Bloodless Bob who muttered gutturally to himself.

Finding a table in a corner we formed a little island on our own, conversing together on matters of mutual interest.

Later, however, buoyed up by ale, we began to glance around the, by then, less-full bar. It was Bloodless Bob's turn to buy a round and he went up to the bar. The landlady, a large woman of middle years, failed to break-off her animated conversation with an obviously valued customer.

Affronted, not unreasonably, by this, Bob reacted perhaps a little uncouthly.

"Here!" he shouted, "put some drinks in here, you daft old cow!"

The immediate reaction from a middle-aged, stickily built man, seated nearby on a bar-stool, was indignant.

"Ah, don't you speak to the lady like that!" he complained, in a Northern Irish accent.

Bob, never one to quail or hesitate at violence, immediately delivered a mighty blow to the Irish man's chin, sending him crashing to the ground.

To his credit, however, he rose wordlessly from the floor and remounted the bar-stool. He stared malevolently at Bob. The landlady, who had not observed the occurrence, so deep was she in conversation, coldly served the drinks to Bob, who resumed his seat with us.

It was not long, however, when he became aware of the Irish man's continued stare fixed upon him.

Without more ado he jumped from his chair and yet again, with one blow, unseated the man.

This time, seemingly offended at his treatment, the Irish man observed: "Ah sure, you've yerself to blame – I'm going to fetch back a few young fellas who'll sort yous out, be God."

138

With that he finished his drink and left.

Old Joe, with the wisdom of age, realised what was likely to happen if the men came back and the pub was wrecked.

"Im *Jallin'* (going) he declared. "If we stops here and he comes back seven or eight-handed, we'll be *kerred* (done) and probably *lelled* (arrested, taken) as well."

After a little though we all agreed, except Bob, the instigator of the trouble, who once outside suddenly went berserk and commenced to grab empty barrels from a nearby stack, casting them with abandon through the windows – breaking both window panes and frames. So fearsome was his attack that none ventured forth from the pub to offer remonstrations.

Eventually daunted by the protests of Benjie he ceased his assault on the building, swearing heartily into the night air until he was, at last, hauled into the motor and we drove away, all more or less intact in spirit.

I felt it would be a relief when we had removed ourselves from the area and the possibility of vengeance.

It should have remained fixed in my memory that it was a rare event indeed for Bloodless Bob to pass an evening peacefully in any public house had he consumed more than two pints of beer. His nature was so aggressive and violent that such a small intake of alcohol would render him psychotic. Legend had it that he was barred from every public house in the Midlands. From my own experiences of his behaviour I had no reason to doubt it. In an organised fight his skills were negligible. He was by nature a bar-room brawler of great ferocity.

One of his nephews, known as 'Tyson,' was even worse. A tall well-built young man in his twenties it took only *one* pint of beer to transpose his mood from genial goodwill to that of a homicidal maniac, expressing a wish to fight anyone in sight for any sum of money they cared to wager. Such, however, was his animal-like contortion of feature, combined with his physical stature, that takers were thin on the ground, everyone but his mother being terrified of him if he had consumed a drink.

It was just past eleven when we got home to the lay-by, and it was unanimously agreed that we would make an early start the next morning in case the police had been alerted of the evening's fracas.

The next morning dawned grey and damp, a thin drizzle sweeping across the low-lying Gloucestershire countryside.

Feeling a little hung-over, and the women all rather out of temper, it did not promise to be a journey of unadulterated pleasure, despite the entire family issuing glowing descriptions of the destination. It was a

139

regular stopping-place, situated by a river we were told, in which those inclined could swim in safety, or fish if the fancy took them.

"A lovely place," Old Joe assured me. "I could bide there for ever."

There could be no greater advertisement I felt.

By Old Joe's reckoning it lay not very far from the town of Pontypool, beside the River Usk. Not, as Benjie had claimed, quite near to Cardiff. It was not a part of Wales to which I had hitherto been tempted. The only possible advantage lay in the fact that it was somewhere new to us.

Eventually taking the Monmouth road from Gloucester and turning off on the Newport road towards Pontypool, we were overtaken by two young men driving a brand new J-type Bedford lorry, painted flashily in bright red and white, the tell-tale step-shaped tow-bar much in evidence.

"Gaahn Gypsies!" they shouted jokily as they passed, blowing their two-note horn musically the while.

It was, at that time, the ambition of every Traveller to come into possession of such a vehicle. With its racy lines, roomy cab, and revolutionary shape it transformed the aspect of almost all 'commercials' from then onwards. It was not until late 1964 that Beshlie and I enjoyed its luxuries when, after three years with the 'lucky' old A-type, we had saved up enough to buy one. It was, I believe, our most exciting and rewarding purchase. Finished in both metallic-bronze, and gold, with an oak panelled body, it was unashamedly 'Travellery' – in the most refined of ways.

We went up to Epsom Downs for Derby Week in 1965 in it – a brand new Jubilee 'Butterfly' trailer completing our turnout.

Everyone wanted to buy the lorry from me – from the colourful 'old-fashioned' Welsh Travellers to those who imagined themselves following a more elevated form of existence.

It was, however, not in my mind to 'chop' away my newest and most-prized object just then: in fact, it remained in our hands for two years, when the days of the J-type were in decline upon the advent of the Ford Transit, and the Bedford C.F.

It was a few hours, and after traversing some harrowingly narrow roads after we had left the main highways, that we found ourselves on a wide green, some thirty or so yards from the bank of the River Usk. The sun was, by then, shining and few, if any, persons contaminated the scene.

We pulled into almost a semi-circle, all our doors facing the river in unison, neither too close nor too distant from each other: I was relieved to note that Bob had managed to insert his trailer in between Letty and Little Joe – some distance from us.

As soon as we had unhitched the trailers and established ourselves both Benjie and Little Joe donned swimming trunks and sped across to the river, launching themselves into its depths with abandon and laughter.

Having never seen Benjie stripped to the waist before I was much impressed by the muscularity of his physique: it is no longer seemed surprising that he had easily over-powered Bloodless Bob. It was apparent, too, that Little Joe would shortly fill-out and run him a close second. Young Joe was devoting himself to attending to some slight malfunction of the innards of his lorry so chose not to so disport himself just then.

Bob lay on the ground staring soulfully in the direction of Letty and the children, who all remained stoically unmoved. They were all too familiar with his ways.

Television was still a comparative rarity amongst Travellers, and even those who owned one were content with a small battery operated set, run from a cable to their motors, and, of course, in black and white. (It was to be 1965 before Beshlie and myself possessed such a luxury.) None of the others were so equipped, so envy did not rear its ugly head. Our communication with the outside world relied upon the recently improved Transistor Radio – the batteries of which could be depended on for months at a time.

For the sixteen years old bride of Little Joe it seemed to be a lease of life, and she played it from dawn till dusk. Her favourite station being Radio Luxembourg, whose output appeared to consist only of contemporary popular music. She rather charmingly referred to it as 'Radio Luckybird' and would sing in accompaniment whenever her favourite ballads were played. Her voice was clear and sweet so it was no hardship for her captive audience.

When encouraged to revert to ancient Romani songs, of which she knew a surprising number, she would complain:

"I cain't a-bear they old-fashioned songs – I likes the new uns."

Sad but inescapable.

As usual I followed the principle; when in Rome do as the Romans do. Hence, like all the others, I decided to 'go on the iron-cart,' as scrap-metal collection was euphemistically termed. Benjie had told me of the presence of a scrapyard in Pontypool who welcomed

Travellers as a source of their supplies, and whose payment was above average.

All that remained was the arduous task of scavenging for saleable materials. In strange country no easy task, I knew. However, I set out the next morning, as did the others, with high hopes of success.

In most families there is usually one outstandingly lucky member, and in this family it was Benjie.

"If my Benjie was to drive into a green field he'd come out with a load of iron," asserted Old Joe to me proudly of his son.

Indeed, in the coming days I was to be faced with evidence of his abilities, unfailingly and regularly. When the rest of us returned daily with but a few hundred-weight of scrap to show for our efforts we would invariably be confronted with the two-ton lorry of Benjie loaded to the gunwales, often with the highest grade of cast-iron or steel-plate off-cuts. Whether bribery and corruption or merely persuasiveness effected these achievements one could only guess.

The days calling in that part of South Wales I found thoroughly dispiriting; the seeming air of unrelieved poverty was oppressive and one could not but wish to be elsewhere.

However, after less than a week beside the River Usk our little cocoon of unity was to fall asunder in a quite dramatic fashion. It was on the Friday evening that, as usual, we left for our visit to a local public house, one near enough to be within walking distance of the trailers. On a Friday, with no work the next day, our beer consumption was generally greater than during the week – with the consequent danger of trouble flaring ahead, particularly from Bloodless Bob, whose two-pint limit would undoubtedly be exceeded with careless disregard for the consequences.

In the bar that evening was a remarkably tall and largely built man, in his thirties one would judge, who seemed fascinated at our little party, nodding and smiling, and obviously anxious to become an active interlocutor in our midst. All through the evening his heavy form leaned over our table, despite our obvious unwillingness to include him in our conversation which, as ever, was devoted solely to Traveller matters.

Eventually Bob, whose aggression was surfacing by the minute, announced, under his breath;

"If this *Gaujo* feller don't fuck off I'm gonna *pogger* (break) every fuckin' bone in his body, s' help me God I is!"

By that time the beer intake was beginning to take its toll on the judgement of us all, so we offered little discouragement to the threats of Bob.

142

Hence our astonishment was not great when he suddenly jumped to his feet, seized a full bottle of beer and broke it over the big man's head, causing a mixture of blood and brown ale to trickle down his moonlike features.

By that time there were but few of the local drinkers left in the bar, and those who *were* there gave no assistance to the large man. To our surprise he offered no retaliation but stood, gazing with the incomprehension of a backward child at his attacker – whom he might well have misguidedly looked on previously as his friend. From no angle was it an example of human nature in its best.

By that time the landlord and landlady, both proudly Welsh though solid-looking and careworn, had begun to issue what could only be construed as a direct invitation to leave. Turning out time, in the literal sense had arrived.

Once outside in the cool night air a chaos of emotions ensued. Old Joe, well over his alcoholic limits, was showing colours which I had never known to be part of his nature.

"See yous!" he shouted, voice slurred and contemptuous, "I could buy you all out ..... or I could *burn* you out!   I got more money than any of you boys'll ever see....I could buy yous all out, an' still have plenty of *loover* (money) left, don't you worry about that."

This outburst, to my surprise, was met with more reaction from Benjie than the others.

"Don't say that, Daddy," he beseeched, his expression close to tears.

Old Joe, however, was too far gone to consider retraction, and continued to hurl abuse at all, but especially at Benjie, who I had always presumed to be his favourite son.

Stumbling homewards, Old Joe continuing his abuse, Benjie endeavouring to pacify him, and Little Joe offering a spirited rendition of the country song 'Poor Boy,' the air was rent with a cacophonous din, unfamiliar, one imagined, to the denizens of the area.

Listening to the song of Little Joe I was not aware of how badly matters had deteriorated between Benjie and Old Joe – smarmily backed-up by Bob – when I heard the old man's voice, shouting in fury and Benjie replying in distress.

".......and you can fuck off with your friend. Just fuck off with your friend, or I'll burn you both out...."

There was no doubt that 'your friend' meant me, and that a long-felt grudge over his son's success had surfaced in the distorted mind of Old Joe.

Upon reaching the trailers I found it was past midnight, and the row showed no sign of abating.

Hurt and injured badly by such an attack from his father, Benjie announced that, despite the hour, he would pack-up there and then and leave.

"Once me dad's like that there's no talking to him," he declared. If I don't go he'll come round with a sledge-hammer and beat the things up – is you coming with me?" Tears rolled down his cheeks.

There was not time for consideration, so I agreed at once.

Beshlie, faced with the unwelcome situation, nonetheless agreed that we had little choice.

So, with as much speed as we could muster, we packed our belongings and pulled-out from the River Usk – neither one of us having the benefit of rear lights on our trailers.

Luckily it was almost full moon so at least our journey was not as hazardous as would have been the case had there been a greater darkness overhead.

A mile or two from the Usk we pulled on to a narrow layby to discuss our destination. After but a few minutes we decided to head for Oxford, a city which we had both found lucky for earning money on past sojourns within its boundaries.

"Let's try the old cattle market," suggested Benjie, naming a stopping-place then much frequented by Travellers, whereon one could usually rely upon five or six days before being moved-on. For some reason it was a favoured resting place for both Irish and Welsh Travellers. For the latter it was convenient for their women to go *dukkering* (fortune-telling) around the nearby City and its environs. In that era, and through the 'seventies and 'eighties it was mainly the efforts of the women in that occupation that supported their families, providing them with food and clothing, not to mention splendidly rococo trailers and lorries.

"Once any man marries one of our women he can cock his legs up for the rest of his life," I was once assured by such a Welsh Traveller. Later, however, they doubled their incomes as more and more of the menfolk started to 'go out,' either scrap-metal seeking, or tarmac-laying.

By sheer good fortune we completed the journey without encountering a single nocturnal police patrol – who would surely have taken exception to our lack of rear illumination, or even to our tax-free lorries!

Soon after we had approached Oxford on the Botley road we swung off, around to the old cattle-market. To our relief there were

144

only about four trailers there, almost certainly Welsh by the look of their immaculate turnouts. Also the Irish Travellers were usually found in larger groups of a dozen or so (one particular family, dealers in antiques then, but later to move into the selling of three-piece suites, were so gregarious that it was not uncommon to see them stopping together with as many as fifty or sixty trailers).

We pulled about thirty or forty yards away from them, the morning light just beginning to show. Debilitated by absence of any sleep our only desire was for rest and slumber: a dubious achievement in such busy surroundings.

Benjie's children had slept during the move so were not as exhausted as their parents or ourselves, and scooted curiously about their new surroundings, disinterested as their mother called to them:

"Mind the varmints! There's long-tails an' all sorts around them old crates an' oil drums!"

Long-tails (rats)

The children received this warning placidly and continued their investigations.

Beshlie and I, in those surroundings, resorted to the gas cooker within the trailer, preparing ourselves a scanty breakfast, before collapsing exhausted upon the bed to try to catch some sleep. Benjie and his wife followed the same course, leaving their children to their explorations – safe in the knowledge that they would not stray far from the trailer: their training had been sound.

After what seemed a very short space of time, however, we found ourselves awoken by the sound of men's voices nearby, unmistakeably those of Welsh Travellers, harsh yet lilting in their tones.

Struggling up I peered through the window and perceived the figures of Old Chasey, his son, and son-in-law, all staring at our turnouts in an effort to identify us.

"God kill me!" exclaimed Old Chasey, excitedly. "It's Benjie, Old Joe's boy, an' the Lone Ranger – I knows his lorry."

Old Chasey had given me the nickname, but thankfully it had never really caught on.

"Well, aye, Uncle Chasey," agreed his son-in-law Mose, tactfully.

Both Old Chasey and his son Young Chasey were short, heavily built, round as dumplings, and of amiable disposition unless provoked severely. The son-in-law was of the same breed, being a kind of second cousin to them. As with many members of their extended families the custom of marrying not too distant relations had created a unique society of like minds and bodies – recognisable at once to those of cognizance, wherever they might be encountered.

From the 1950s to the 1980s such families became more and more visible. This was to some extent due to their endearing combination of the old-fashioned with newest products of trailers and lorries and cooking on outside *yogs* (fires). Stopping exclusively on commons, roadsides, laybys or car-parks, for just a few days at a time, travelling over almost all of the country, theirs seemed indeed to be 'the gypsy life.' Until as late as the 'nineties it was no uncommon sight to see their splendidly ornate Vickers or Westmorland Star trailers, drawn by J-type or TK Bedford lorries so encamped. Alas, such freedom could not be allowed to last; gradually persecution and imagined good-intentions succeeded in their aim of destroying such a life-style. The Mini-Reservations (or Council Sites as they are called) were provided, and slowly all such itinerant families were either forced or persuaded to adopt a life quite foreign to them.

To me it just becomes depressing that a whole mode of existence, satisfying and rewarding to those within it, has virtually been wiped out within so short a space of time. Whenever I meet people from such families, all forced on to sites, their nostalgic memories of their past lives, free and exciting, are fulsomely expressed. If, in years to come, the present site-dwellers are placed in council houses I cannot imagine them being nostalgic for the life on closed-in sites, hidden away behind high-walls to protect the sensitivities of the public.

At that time, however, the way of life was still developing. The market for more than previously ornately decorated trailers, produced exclusively for Travellers, was being exploited to the full – inflation and manufacturing costs rose so steeply that the two main players were forced to withdraw from the competition. The succeeding firms who attempted to invade the market never managed to approach the magnificence of either Vickers or Westmorland Star. Cheaper and less imposing in design they never received the stature of their predecessors.

Emerging sleepily from the trailer I faced the trio in a somewhat dazed condition.

"My dear old kid," observed Old Chasey. "Was you *asutti* (asleep)?" he enquired solicitously.

"That's all right, my Old Chasey," I replied. Adding for his titillation: "We had a bit of trouble in Wales last evening – so we thought it best to *jal* (go)."

Too polite to ask for details they nodded sagely amongst themselves. "I just turns round and walks away – once it starts it won't stop, like my dear old father always said."

"Well, aye, man," agreed Young Chasey, lighting a small cigar, exhaling strongly over his father and brother-in-law which set them simultaneously coughing.

"How long've you been here, Chasey?" I enquired.

"We *avved* (came) here a-Sunday – no one ain't bin to us, so I should think we'll catch another few days. One of the market-men's a lamb an' the other's a *beng!* (devil)," replied Young Chasey, whilst the other two nodded solemnly in agreement.

Despite, like most of his breed, possessing natural good manners and restraint, Old Chasey found it impossible to avoid prying into the cause of the 'trouble.'

"Was Old Joe there?" he asked innocently. "And that Bob?" he further enquired. Upon my admitting their presence he nodded wisely.

"See them two? If they gets together in a *kitchemir* there's bound to be trouble of one sort or another – you can bet on it."

His son and son-in-law both fervently agreed.

"See Benjie," remarked Young Chasey, "he's the nicest feller in the world – he'd give you the heart out of his body if you needed it. You couldn't fault the man, ain't that right, Mose?"

"Sure it is," confirmed Mose. "It's that Bob who generally causes the fighting – Benjie an' him can't a-bear each other, never could. Even before Benjie put him in hospital – the only man to beat him, by all accounts."

"Having a busy day?" I enquired jokily, trying to change the subject.

"Well aye, kid – I should think so," grinned Old Chasey.

"The women's all out *dukkerin'* an' *bikkinin'* (selling) a bit of lace to try an' git a bit've *loover* (money). Us'll just sit down on our *buls* (posteriors) till they gits back with a bit of bread and meat – not too late, I hopes."

There is no doubt in my mind, after having spent spasmodic periods of time with the likes of Old Chasey and his scattered relatives, from Cornwall to Scotland, that the form of existence that they followed, especially from the '60s to the '80s, were wholly admirable in almost every way: pride, comparative wealth, and freedom of spirit were its finest attributes.

That they have been driven from the waysides is a little tragedy of our times.

After a few more minutes they withdrew to their fire and I set about a bacon sandwich and a cup of tea before starting out in an effort to earn a day's work after lean times around the River Usk. Owing to the autumnal season I felt it might be a good idea to explore the Compost Trail, hopefully to reap substantial rewards from the well-healed academics who thronged in and around the City of Oxford. For many of whom gardening was their relaxation.

Knowing the Oxford environs quite well it was with but little difficulty that I cudgelled my memory into reviving the addresses of both empty feed-bag suppliers, and also the equine establishments who would be more than relieved to have their ever growing heaps of rotting ordure removed by the likes of myself.

I even called to mind the name of an infinitely bribe-able gardener at one of the most famous colleges. In the past, five pounds in his hand resulted in fifty pounds in mine – such was the trust that the gullible academics placed in their employee, whose blatant financial advancement was his main aim in life. To me, of course, he was a valuable find, whose goodwill I cushioned close to my chest. To my great amusement I found out later that he was a respected lay-preacher in one of the well-known religious splinter groups that seem to flourish widely among the needy, misguided, or lunacy fringe.

As our relationship was purely of a business nature I did not allow it to prejudice me against him. Indifference was my clothing.

After having performed the arduous labour of filling up some fifty bags of manure at a small riding school on the outskirts of the City I decided to try the college gardener.

I found him seated in a shed enjoying a sandwich and a cigarette. His expression barely altered on sighting me, apart from a slight rolling of his eyes beneath the peak of his cap."

"It's all right for you," I smiled encouragingly.

"All right for you, more'n likely," he rejoined. "You got some more of that muck as you wants to poke on me, I suppose – how many have you got aboard?"

"Fifty, like you had last time I called – at the same price, with a nice little drink in it for you. I know they go on your recommendation."

His watering eyes brightened slightly.

"I'll go and see the Bursar – he'll want a receipt, mind," he said, leaving his shed, with the promise of his speedy fulfilment.

Sure enough he returned within five minutes, his face impassive.

"Ar, that's all right then, he'll take 'em on my word. You gimme the same as before, all right? An' we'll put 'em over there in the corner by the wall," he said, gesturing to the place he favoured, which fortunately was spacious enough to allow me to reverse the lorry in close for ease of off-loading. The latter exercise was eased by lethargic assistance from a gormless youth, who was apparently a delinquent of sorts, enjoying the benefits of a course generously provided for a limited number of his ilk, snatched at random from the city streets, with the hopes that their natures might be improved by enforced dedication to the soil and its products. The aim was good, I felt, but the reasoning a trifle optimistic.

The gardener himself remained aloof from the off-loading, merely devoting himself to directing the unwilling youth and myself as to the exact location that he required each bag to be stationed. However, curiously energised by the prospect of receiving a cash payment my speed of work reached almost Olympic standards. Hence within a matter of fifteen minutes my lorry was emptied and I was on my way to the Bursary for my pay out. The Bursar himself, a scholarly and unusually polite man, had prepared a detailed receipt for me to examine and, upon obtaining of my signature, counted out the requisite sum without any hesitation. His occupation as Pay Master did not appear to have had any deleterious effects on his nature: unusual in my experience. The whole matter was graciously concluded in no time.

Thus, gathering up the money I left the office, heading off to present the gardener with his 'drink' in gratitude for his, to a large extent, engineering the transaction.

With the achievement of a 'one hit' so early in the day the tensions left me temporarily – only to be revived on my next day of 'calling.' Unhealthy for the placid or lazy perhaps, but for me and those of a similar nature it is the stress and the tension that activates the dynamo of one's personality.

Oxford at that time was on the brink of the 1960s revolution in clothing, hair-styles, and sexual mores: a wondrous amalgam of long repressed human behaviour. I suppose that in Oxford it was more excitingly on display than in more conservative cities and towns, for the time being. Suddenly, as though overnight, the students, particularly, became transformed from their grimly drab appearances, both boys and girls, into exotic creatures from another planet, both sexes bejewelled, be-robed, and generously addicted to hair. The men sported interesting challenges to the hitherto universal 'short back and sides': an ugly fashion, still finding approbation in the eyes of the tri-striped soldiery.

For both Beshlie and myself it was, apart from the rising consumption of 'substances,' our natural habitat. To be constantly confronted by such exotica was, in my view anyway, a considerable bonus for the eye. Without doubt the 1960s became my favourite decade. During it I grew up: a novel experience indeed. It almost brought about the mythical belief that the freedom for which our fathers battled had eventually been achieved. How sad was that?

I treated myself to a modestly splendid, if lone, lunch at one of the new and rather informal restaurants that were opening almost everywhere. They were usually staffed by pretty young women in casual, even somewhat revealing attire, or young men of over cultivated coiffures and excessively clinging trousers, supercilious of expression, a napkin aboard their arm: the food offered was a far cry from the British Restaurant! In this instance I chose a dish of mixed vegetable curry, which proved to be of an exceptionally scented and spiced make-up: I had not tasted a more enticing dish in any other establishments where I had eaten – apart from one occasion at a five-star hotel where I had been guest of an American millionaire and his wife. However, upon this day I restricted myself to a single course followed by Turkish coffee. I seem to remember receiving quite substantial change from a five pound note!

Upon returning to the cattle market by midday I was not entirely astonished to see that our numbers had grown.

Five more trailers had pulled-in not long since, and their owners were making themselves at home.

I recognised the group as being Boggy Lee, two of his married sons, a married daughter, and her father-in-law, Old Jack Taylor. I was delighted to see them as they were all sensible and affable people, the best of company. They were second cousins to Old Chasey and as such were completely immersed in matters concerning their mutual and innumerable relatives, most of whom in those times were still on the roads and mainly prospering within their own capabilities, some to an astonishing degree.

Boggy and Jack were then in their early fifties, but their faces carried the lines and weariness generally not so obvious until a more advance age. Both had been born in waggons and had, when first married, retained that way of life: each had surrendered to mechanisation only within the past decade or so. Their wives were sisters and had been used to going out 'calling' with their mothers and aunts from a very early age: hence with such good training when so young they were each well-equipped to provide their own families, once they had married, with a high standard of living. During those years their womenfolk still clung to the old-fashioned 'gypsy look' in both their braided hair and long dresses, shawls, and head-scarves. To see them set off each morning, like a flock of colourful birds, laughing and chattering, young and old, was a great pleasure, and a considerable comfort to the likes of myself.

Within the group, just then, I was the only man going out and earning money, which seemed a little strange.

It was, however, no few years further when the men of those families, and most of their relatives, revolutionised their previous existences by the act of commencing to earn money themselves. Following, in some cases, the Traveller-style occupations of tarmac-laying and tree-topping, most seemed to veer towards the field of non ferrous scrap metal collection – which appeared to come as second nature to them.

The newcomers came with three Eccles Traveller trailers, each nearly new, one Siddal trailer, coach-built and solid; whilst the other was an 18ft Berkeley. The latter was not specifically manufactured for Travellers, having no extra adornments of 'flash' in its design. Its one attraction being its built-in solid fuel stove: at that period all Travellers' trailers were so provided. A home was not a home without a wood and coal burning stove!

With the arrival of the newcomers the number of children grew to a dozen or more. They ranged in years from babes in arms to, in the case of the girls, their early teens. The eldest of the boys seeming to be nor more than ten or twelve. Those from the age of about five or six onwards were almost all clad in little tailor-made suits and either cloth caps or little trilby hats, thus attempting to become miniatures of their fathers, even sporting diminutive jodhpur boots in tan or yellow leather. Their paths in life were already laid out for them – surely a basis of security.

Old Jack Taylor was one of nature's gentlemen, polite and generous in manner. A fine figure of a man, with coal-black hair and eyes, he stood over six feet in height, solidly built. In his younger days, I was told, he had been a bare-knuckle fighting champion in the valleys of South Wales. But by the time I met him he had become quieter, long retired from pugilism. His wife was a close relative of Old Chasey's wife so they were pleased to be in each other's company – even if only for a day or two.

The owner of the Siddal trailer was a son-in-law of Jack and a nephew of Old Chasey. Named Spinney he was a 'lucky' young man, his earning capacity seemed unlimited. Assisted by the *dukkering* prowess of his wife they were in an enviable position for so young a couple. Indeed within only a few more years Spinney had his first brand new Rolls Royce. If one should visit them, on a roadside or an old common, it was heart-warming to witness the immaculate limousine parked beside a splendid new trailer and lorry – whilst Spinney and his wife and small children sat around a stick-fire eating their food. It was such a combination of the modern and the old-fashioned that I found so pleasing. Black cooking pots, kettles, kettle-cranes, and *chitties* (tripods) were an essential part of their luggage, and that of most of their relatives.

Boggy and Jack, although still only in their fifties, represented a fast fading class of Traveller, both in their behaviour and expression. They were of the old-fashioned inward-looking mentality: little of anything outside the Romani world concerned them. To some extent it was, perhaps, the hardships and prejudices forced on them from the outside world that drove them so to be. In some ways, of course, their outlook was advantageous to them, increasing their awareness of the closeness of their existence with their fellows.

"Is the water-taps still working?" called Jack to Old Chasey.

"Well, aye man," replied the latter emphatically. Adding for effect: "Even in the frost he's all right once he's un-thawed – an' in the afternoons the *pani* (water) comes out freezing hot!"

Seemingly unfazed by the curiosity of Old Chasey's reply Jack merely nodded.

Soon Old Jack and Spinney returned to their trailers, their lorry backs loaded with three or four milk-churns of water from the convenient tap. Both then proceeded to wash-down their trailers and lorries after their journey: a practice to which most Travellers are addicted – or certainly those with pride in their possessions.

At about seven-thirty that evening I was invited by Old Jack to join himself, Old Chasey, Young Chasey and Boggy for "a quiet drink at The Ferret." The last named was a humble inn within easy walking distance from the Cattle Market, the landlady of which was not generally averse to the presence of Travellers on her premises.

Even though our destination was of no social elevation all of us donned our best suits for the outing. The older men sported hats and suits the younger favoured leather jackets and slicked-back hair styles. I had just obtained a smartly tailored black leather jacket, yoke-backed and multi-pocketed. With narrow black trousers and elastic-sided boots I felt equal to the occasion. (I was never one to 'dress down' with Travellers. I leave that to social workers – who innocently imagine it endears them to their 'clients.')

We reached The Ferret after a less than five--minutes' walk. The interior was barren, over-scrubbed, and devoid of anything even remotely welcoming in its atmosphere. Leatherette benches ran along two walls and two or three bare tables and uncomfortable-looking chairs were placed about the room. It was one of the few public-houses that I have visited where there was neither Lounge nor Saloon Bar: its repertoire was limited to a single room.

We drew two tables together and settled ourselves in a corner, seated on the benches, our filled glasses on the tables in front of us – accompanied by half a dozen packets of peanuts, generously provided by Young Chasey, for whom some form of food-intake was more or less non-stop.

The landlady, a paunchy woman of middle-age, surprisingly unattractive at a casual glance, proved even more so on closer inspection. Heavily made up in the style of Gloria Swanson on a bad day, chain-smoking and bronchial-sounding, she was little advertisement for the calling she had followed.

Although we were keeping ourselves to ourselves, enjoying a game of dominoes – with the 'penny a spot' variation for small stakes, her eyes rarely left us: we were under scrutiny.

At about nine-thirty, by which time we were improved in spirit but by no means drunk, our little group was suddenly invaded by two young house-dwelling Travellers who lived nearby. Known as Pinky and Perky they were brothers, notorious in the area for their fighting, *choring* (stealing), and outrageous behaviour: they enjoyed little popularity in either the Travellers' world nor that of the *Gaujes*. However, each being over six feet tall and apparently without any form of fear or respect, their company was rarely welcomed. They were con-men of the first order, with a studied choice of garments that were aimed to distance them from the gypsy-look in every way. They both wore well-cut hacking jackets of restrained colouration, cavalry-twill trousers and suede boots. Their shirts were of tattersall check and their ties (a rarity amongst Travellers) were of paisley patterned silk; everything was geared to inspiring confidence in the eyes of the wealthy inhabitants of Oxford and its environs. Only their voices gave them away, rough and harsh, though even those tones were moderated by them into what they fondly imagined was middle-class when calling. Unfortunately, however, their grasp of grammar was scant and they tended to fail dismally in their vocal intentions if confronted by anyone of even a slightly discerning nature. Nonetheless, despite such occasional disasters, they seemed to have an inborn ability to seek out victims of an especially gullible nature. Their form of off-stage acting never failed to impress me. Only their extraordinarily unsuitable nicknames mystified me, but once given to them by some misguided wag it had stuck indelibly to them.

By the time they arrived at The Ferret they were already in a semi-intoxicated state and one sensed that trouble of some sort or another would ensue: our little party exchanging warning looks.

The brothers stood by our table, drinking 'whiskey-Americans' and smoking thin cigars. We did not welcome them too effusively, but did not wish to offend them so smiled hypocritically at them.

Earlier in the evening two dozen eggs had been raffled at the bar, and Spinney had bought each of us a ticket in a fit of eccentric generosity. When the winning ticket number was announced I found to my astonishment, that it was mine. It was a little disheartening for me as I have never eaten eggs.

Thus, with the two containers, each filled with a dozen eggs, set before me I felt it only right to offer them to anyone who desired them.

Such an innocent gesture appeared to enrage the elder brother, Pinky, who without hesitation brought his fist down with extreme force on to the egg-boxes.

The effect was highly dramatic: the containers burst and spurts of egg-yolk splashed over our party and the surrounding walls and tables.

"The Lord fuck the eggs!" shouted Pinky in triumph, wiping his jacket cuff, and grinning evilly upon us.

Old Chasey was worst served, with egg-yolk streaming down his face after a direct hit. All the rest of us were, to a lesser degree, so splattered.

The landlady became like a person possessed, launching herself from behind the bar, purple with fury, demanding our immediate exit from the bar, and the promise that we would never be served there again. Our feelings were a little hurt as we were but victims. Pinky and Perky were the villains, now reduced to uncontrolled laughter by the result of Pinky's imbecilic action.

Despite their advanced state of intoxication the two brothers left in Perky's large new Jaguar limousine, with a squeal of tyres, the radio blaring, and fulsome sounding of the horn emitting a tasteful multi-toned version of Colonel Bogey! (Alas such musical adventures were later banned from usage, a fact bemoaned by some and applauded by the majority.)

"Proper 'ring-tails,'" complained Spinney of the brothers, echoing the opinion of us all.

"Now the *kitchema's* (pub's) fucked an' we'll have to go fifty miles to find another," observed Old Chasey with his normal exaggeration.

Hence it was a rather dejected little group that sauntered homewards, earlier than expected by the surprised womenfolk, for whom 'turning out' time was the norm.

"Cow's cunt and cauliflower for me supper," grinned Old Jack, upon which optimistic note we retired to our respective trailers.

In retrospect I was rather pleased that Benjie had declined our invitation to The Ferret. I knew from experience that his reaction would have been one of instinctive retaliation against the two brothers – without doubt causing a full scale escalation of violence; exciting at the time but invariably having unfortunate repercussions later.

The next morning I consulted with Benjie, describing the events of the previous evening.

"Ring-tails!" he exclaimed in disgust. "If I'd a'bin there I'd 'ave beaten 'em out of the pub, on my baby's life I would."

Benjie was a good friend in most ways; his only drawback being his affection for public-house brawling.

He expressed his desire to try his hand at what was euphemistically known as the 'muck-game.' It was an occupation permanently engaged upon by a few families who did nothing else, its grip upon them seeming unbreakable. Their earnings appeared sufficient for them to afford the latest Traveller possessions. It was, and indeed is, a clean profession in comparison to tarmac-laying, painting, or even tree-topping.

Helping him, in the way that I myself have often received assistance, I explained that I was off to 'bag-up' at a riding stable and suggested that he follow me in his lorry and fulfil the same arduous task. I had found plenty of old feed bags at a farm nearby so offered him some to set him up for the day.

In those times, still young and energetic, I thought nothing of filling fifty or even sixty bags for a day's calling. One advantageous spur to selling in paper bags, as opposed to plastic, was the knowledge that it was imperative to dispose of them the same day, otherwise disaster followed owing to the fact that the bags would disintegrate and leak their contents about suburbia – with decidedly unprofitable results. The daily slavery of 'bagging-up' was the main handicap to the occupation.

(Few, I suppose, could boast that one of their highest achievements is to have 'bagged-up' manure from St Ives in Cornwall to Aberdeen in Scotland! But the boast is mine.)

Benjie seemed pleased by my suggestion, and within half an hour we were alongside each other, our lorry backs confronting an enticing-looking midden of mature horse manure. I had my own fork and Benjie borrowed one from the slightly decayed-looking old gentlewoman who owned the premises and most of the dozen or so horses in the adjacent loose boxes. A variety of fetching young women appeared to be on her pay-roll as stable-girls, a fact not lost on Benjie who was enthused by their various physical assets, generously sharing his conclusions with me. Such speculations would not, however, buy the baby a new frock nor assist in the job to hand; a fact eventually absorbed by Benjie when he found that I had completed forty bags before he had filled twenty. His was not the single-mindedness which is paramount in the success of the businessman – no matter how lowly that business may be.

The next five days passed quietly, my dedication to the compost-trail paying dividends of an unexpected level. The academics of Oxford, pining perhaps for idyllic rusticity, were more than grateful to receive my attentions. Alas, however, our peace was shattered by the arrival of several families of Irish Travellers, of a rather bombastic nature, with uncontrolled children and dogs: we would have preferred their room to their company. Also with their swelling of the numbers to excess, it was only a matter of hours before our departure was demanded by the 'devilish' natured market official – backed-up by four policemen.

Our immediate move was at first ordered; but after prolonged cajoling's from Old Chasey it was postponed until the next morning. Not without heavy threats of intrusive action from the authorities if we were still ensconced there.

We would have to go; there was little argument to that.

After prolonged discussion we decided to split up. The Irish were a world of their own – their destination of no moment to us – the rest of us, however, taking different roads. Old Chasey and his family decided to make for Buckinghamshire, whilst Old Jack was heading for Devon – which was something of a temptation for me as I am fond of that county.

Eventually, however, Benjie and I agreed upon the idea of Brighton. He had not been to that part of the country but I knew that he would be taken by the atmosphere, of Brighton: it had always been one of my favourite cities.

Our final decision was to make the journey in two or three stages. The first stop to be just outside Newbury, maybe calling at a few likely houses that had remained in my mind. From thence to Winchester, by-passing Southampton and heading along the A27 coastal road towards Brighton, around the environs of which I was familiar with a number of stopping-places where-on one might snatch a few days, and also a rather unprepossessing piece of litter-strewn wasteland upon which time-limits were rarely set. Indeed, some 'rough' local Travellers had remained there, static for a number of years – naturally incurring wrath and displeasure in the minds of local residents, whose vocal outbursts were regularly given printed airing in the local newspaper. Happily without much apparent effect at that time.

Our old lorry, then approaching its eighth year, was still performing admirably, giving no reason to question the reputation of the legendary Bedford. Apart from a thirst for oil almost equal to its need for petrol, it continued to serve us well.

However, as my prosperity had grown, relatively speaking, I felt that the time for improvement was nigh.

We had saved sufficient money to be able to afford a brand new J-type Bedford lorry, providing that a deal could be struck over part-exchange for 'Pig's Head's' vehicle. Time would tell.

Within three days we had accomplished the journey to our destination. Attention from unsympathetic police at both Newbury and Winchester encouraged us to push on towards Chichester and then Worthing, where we found a reasonably situated lay-by upon which we stayed for two days, recouping our expenses by a day 'muck-hawking' around the suburbs of the genteel town, somewhat to the relief of both Beshlie and Marie – the latter sharing Beshlie's leaning towards pessimism.

After discussion I persuaded Benjie that it might be wisest to head for Ditchling Common, where-on I knew we could stop without any fear of eviction. The local 'rough' Travellers permanently in residence there, under the auspices of their ancient patriarch Banjo Bob, were usually amicably disposed to strangers pulling-on, provided their numbers were not too great. Fresh company was something of a novelty to them. In the past I had found them pleasant and friendly, though severely localised in outlook. Sussex and its extremities comprised their knowledge of the world. Such insularity had its own charm.

The main disadvantage of Ditchling Common lay in its distance from the city of Brighton – probably a dozen or more miles at least. Nearer, though, the prosperous little towns of Burgess Hill and Haywards Heath were both enticing opportunities for calling and earning money, but neither town possessed the raffish and exciting character of Brighton.

From Worthing it was no great journey to the common, which I found largely unchanged in character from the time of my last sojourn amidst its rubbish-strewn fastness. Hence we were able to establish ourselves upon an oil-slicked patch, surrounded by low and withered bushes, possibly a hundred yards from the group that comprised the family of Banjo Bob. Over to our right, on a patch of ground similar to our own, perhaps fifty yards distant, sat one small, tidily painted, trailer and a Fordson truck of no great age. Like the trailer it was smartly-painted in a pleasing crimson, lined-out in straw colour: there was about the little turnout an air of pride and respectability – considerably at odds with the neglected and ramshackle vehicles of Banjo Bob's family. The owner was distantly related to the families of Banjo Bob, but followed his own slightly elevated path, still itinerant and proud of the fact. It was Joey, with Ida and their two small children. Our paths had crossed before, in Kent.

We were soon unpacked, Benjie's children scavenging about in the surrounding stunted bushes accompanied by Benjie's two deerhound-greyhound lurchers.

There was little 'natural' wood to be found, but luckily some beneficent local builder had dumped a huge pile of old beams and rotted floorboards nearby which provided us with a goodly supply for our *yogs*. Like ourselves Benjie was dedicated to cooking on an outside fire, with the universal Traveller assertion that food so prepared retained a finer flavour than that cooked inside the trailers on stoves fuelled by 'bottled' gas.

Fortunately no members of Banjo Bob's family strayed over to us: their reaction to our presence being tinged with envy at our mobility, and tinged with shame at their own almost sedentary existence. Their position was not to be admired: looked down on by itinerant Travellers, and despised as being 'not real gypsies' by the local inhabitants. The latter, with unrivalled ferocity, blamed them for all the rubbish being constantly deposited about the common by *Gaujo* 'fly-tippers' of uncaring natures.

At that time their little settlement consisted of several old hardboard trailer-caravans, a few makeshift sheds, a couple of bender tents, and an old decaying Open Lot waggon in which resided the elderly Banjo Bob, solitary since the death of his ancient wife not long before.

A year or two into the future, when I next stopped there, in the company another Welsh Traveller, Manuel Evans – 'The Latin from Prestatyn.' – the whole of Banjo Bob's family, sons, daughters, and grandchildren, were on the point of being re-housed into council property on a not too distant housing estate. It was the end of the road, their final degradation, and I would not be surprised if they were gradually absorbed into the lower echelons of *Gaujo* life. I never bothered to find out.

I knew where we might find some supplies of compost for our hawking, so we agreed to postpone bagging-up until the following morning, planning to rest lazily after our rather arduous journey from Oxford.

It was probably about four o'clock, we had just finished consuming our 'tea' when we were disturbed by the sight of a well 'flashed-up' A-type Bedford painted scarlet and lined-out. Its body was fitted with high aluminium sides and rear, thus preventing even the most inquisitive spectator to assess the nature of any contents it might be carrying.

"That's me cousin Rudi," exclaimed Benjie. "Where's ever he stopping?"

The lorry drew up and out jumped three men. Rudi was tall and handsome, his appearance enhanced by a head of thick greying hair, black brows, and a drooping black 'Zapata' moustache. The other two were in their late twenties, obviously brothers, each with professionally styled hair, and snappy apparel of fashionable mode. Their tan jodhpur boots being their only concession to Traveller fashion: one of them was yet another brother-in-law if Old Jack, the other un-married. All three carried the same accent: Welsh, yet overlaid with a characteristic lilt, and turn of phrase, which immediately marked them out as members of their incredibly extended family. It was no surprise to learn that one of the young men, Seth, was Rudi's son-in-law, with the other one,

Rainbow, hoping soon to follow the same route with Rudi's youngest daughter.

It transpired that in the back of the lorry were three lurchers and that they were on their way to some downs, not far distant, to run the dogs in the hopes of catching a hare or two. Seeing us unexpectedly they had driven in to invite us to accompany them – a suggestion to which we readily agreed.

Benjie decided to take his older dog, and I to take mine. The latter, a tall saluki-greyhound cross deerhound was an enthusiastic hare-catcher, I knew from experience.

All five dogs were in a state of high excitement and anticipation, realising that a ride in the back of a lorry would end in a run on the downs. They were tense and enthusiastic, and in no mood for fighting among themselves.

It was with some difficulty that we managed to cram all of us into the cab: luckily tactility was not a thing we feared.

Within five or ten minutes we took a series of back roads and lanes, eventually turning into a hilly rutted track. They had been there before, otherwise it would have been hard to find, as it culminated unexpectedly on to the edge of a vista of Sussex downland – of the kind which must surely have excited the creative juices in the likes of the artist Ivon Hitchens, whose sweeping brush-strokes so readily captured the spirit of such scenes.

Rudi pulled the lorry in against a hedge and we fell out of the cab, beset by cramps and aches. However, such things were soon forgotten and we released the dogs whose hysteria knew no bounds. Within moments we were on the edge of the downs and Rudi pointed far across the afternoon sunlit expanse at a minute dot.

"God kill me! There's one over there – an' two there," he gestured, at distant hares.

I was immediately struck by the animation and energy exuding from both men and dogs, their zeal and enthusiasm a joy to watch. In that moment dog and man were in their true element, in the way that their forbears must have been when hunting food for their very survival. The spirit was still alive, thriving just beneath the surface.

Within seconds the dogs were off, hurtling in the direction of the unwary hares who sere soon outrun. My own dog caught the first, closely followed by Benjie's. Eventually, after several sweeps the remaining hares seemed to comprehend their dangerous predicament and quietly withdrew to lie low until our departure.

The contemporary Animal Rights Activist might, in a fit of pique perhaps, denigrate our actions as being cruel. In an enclosed surrounding with the hare having no chance of escape I would agree. In the open, however, the whole operation seems to me to be in complete synchronization with the tenets of Nature. Both hare and dog become transformed into creatures of beauty in their movement, each performing as instinct dictated. Different indeed from the unspeakable brutality of badger-baiting or dog-fighting: both of which produce nothing of beauty or grace, and little or no chance for the combatants.

As the sun sank lower in the sky we called in the dogs, collected the hares, and loaded the exhausted dogs back on the lorry.

"You got a good dog there, old kid," observed Rudi. "Do you want to sell him?"

Generally not one to turn away an offer I nonetheless refused to put a price on my dog: I had become rather attached to him. But it was nice to be asked! Rudi, who was a man of sunny disposition, accepted my decision placidly.

Our journey homewards was filled with camaraderie and good humour. Who, in their right mind, could find fault with something that engendered such reactions? (Many, I suspect!)

Dropping Benjie and myself and our dogs at our trailers, Rudi and the brothers felt unable to stay for any tea. They were stopping on the coastal road, on a layby near to Lancing, within telescopic view of its esteemed college. They had been there for a week and, apart from a zealous Council Pest Controller, they had been free of persecution by the authorities and considered themselves lucky. Such was the way of life then. Nowadays their departure would have been enforced within twenty-four hours or less.

Benjie and I were in cheerful mood, each carrying a sturdy hare. We agreed to follow our individual paths next morning – the compost trail still beckoning.

Neither of us enquired as to the direction in which we would head; though I fancied Brighton, both for its atmosphere and the fact that I had several 'marks' residing in the surrounding suburbs whose appetite for organic compost appeared unquenchable.

One particularly eccentric buyer was an aged autocratic lady who lived in an old toll house not far from the town. This gentlewoman's singularity was emphasised by the fact that her habitual clothing consisted solely of hessian sacks wrapped about her person, secured at vital points by red binder twine – even her feet were so encased. This outlandish choice of garments was fully matched by the conditions prevailing within the house. The effect of its chaotic interior could only provoke the fancy that some form of celestial power had seized the building, turned it upside down and shaken it, before dumping it roughly, right side up.

On this visit I was able to persuade her to take twelve bags, more than on a previous call a year or so before, on which she demanded that I should leave them inside the front room, against the wall.

Her garden was ahead of its time insofar as she had no apparent realization of the difference between flowers and vegetables, sewing them indiscriminately as the whim took her. It was a theory of horticulture that I once observed, some years later, being employed by the members of a hippy commune in a remote part of Mid-Wales. For the devotee, no doubt, it had its own fascination, and was preferable to the vulgarity of many a suburban garden's displays of odious blooms stationed with military precision about their immaculate borders.

This was a woman whose existence was not hindered by convention nor the seeking of approbation from her fellows. Her mind was sharp, and her ability to haggle over the cost would surely have earned her respect from the average market-trader. Alas her like will never be seen again, and as they vacate this planet there are no replacements to follow them, or certainly not of such dated gentility.

Characteristically, perhaps, the notes that she offered me in payment were of an obsolete issue, not legal tender in fact. However, not allowing such trivialities to cloud my judgement, I readily accepted them without hesitation, knowing that they could be exchanged at any bank. To have declined her payment could have seemed ungracious.

With the remarkable luck than can occasionally strike the hawker on a 'good' day, I managed to dispose of the remainder of my cargo in one 'hit' at the premises of yet another 'mark' with whom I had previously made a sale. This last was a retired Major General who, with an elderly tweed-suited wife, resided in a spacious residence, of a size that could have accommodated two or three families with ease. On this occasion they informed me that they were considering leaving their mansion-like retreat in favour of 'a small flat in Bayswater.' However, as their plans were somewhat fluid they decided to avail themselves of my offer, in case their plans were delayed. They showed me a space at one side of their garage and requested me to stack the bags 'as neatly as possible.' Needless to say they offered me no assistance in the task. And I would not have expected it from such pillars of gentility.

I was nonetheless, somewhat put out as they stood beside me, carefully counting the numbers unloaded.

Only for a moment did they allow their gaze to wander – across the road to the garden of a house of similar proportions to their own. An elderly bald-headed man was guiding a petrol-driven mower about the pasture with an air of fixed concentration.

"Oh!" exclaimed the wife of the Major General. "There's that dreadful German man in his garden – simply frightful!"

I glanced curiously at her and she explained:

"A most terrible man – an ex U-Boat Commander would you believe. His poor wife, he treats her very badly. Many's the time I've seen him *frog-marching* her round the garden! Isn't that right, Roger?"

The Major General grunted a reply, unwilling to conduct a conversation with either his wife or myself.

Once the bags were safely stored I was offered a cheque in payment, as had been the case on my previous visit. It was via the cheque that I was aware of the rank of the person with whom I was dealing. It was signed: Roger Mc........(Major General Retired) as part of the signature. Possibly my life has been sheltered but I have never, before or since, been presented with a cheque so inscribed. However, as in those carefree times one could cash cheques anywhere, with publican or tradesman, I knew that it could do little but inspire confidence in the mind of whoever accepted it. Majors were quite common but 'Major-Generals Retired' were distinctly thin on the ground.

Back on the common by midday, the sun shining in a cloudless sky, even the uninspiring settlement of Banjo Bob's family seemed inoffensive, despite the clouds of acrid black smoke emanating from a heap of rubber-encased copper-cable which one of his sons was burning-off, in order to offer it as 'clean' metal when weighing it in at the local scrap-merchant's yard. In that moment only non-ferrous metals were profitable. Cast-iron, steel, and especially 'light', were commanding such execrable prices that they were scarcely worth collecting. Indeed, the preponderance of old car-bodies, tins, and corrugated-iron sheeting were evidence of the fact, though it was optimistically presumed that the fluctuating market might soon tilt in their favour, Bob's family were natural hoarders, their sense of the aesthetic undeveloped, hence its presence did not cause them dismay.

It was not long before the colourful lorry of Benjie, accompanied by his wife and children, drew in beside his trailer, into which Marie

163

hoisted numerous bags of provisions. The lorry was empty so I concluded that their day had been successful. The inclusion of Marie as an assistant was a wise step as her skills at extracting money from even the most hostile of householders was legendary amongst the other Travellers. Her technique on the doorsteps, an endearing mixture of wheedling and independence, would usually bring its just reward.

On Friday evening, after a well- rewarded few days of calling, Benjie and myself decided to spend an evening in Brighton hoping for a more exciting experience than that offered by village hostelries,

We went in Benjie's lorry, which we left in a car-park on the edge of the city, walking along the street, through the antiques-selling area known as the 'lanes.' We quickly spied a public house of attractive appearance. A large placard beside the entrance to the Lounge Bar assured the placid customer that their lunch times would be enlivened by a number of young ladies who, for their pleasure, were wont to disrobe daily between one and two o'clock.

Benjie, being unable to read or write, was not able to perceive that information. I, however, in an act of charity apprised him of the message.

"Cah! I'll be down here tomorrow morning, child's life I will," he responded enthusiastically.

Since it was well past two o'clock, indeed, nearer to eight, the bar presented a rather forlorn aspect; a small stage at one end was partially concealed by faded leopard-skin printed fabric.

The customers too, at that time of evening, were of distinctly shabby appearance, capped and rain-coated, and absorbing pints of black beer. Two well-built ladies in the early stages of middle-age, were seated together at one end of the bar. Heavily made-up, ravaged of feature, their white cleavages liable to set in motion a condition near to snow-blindness, it did not take a genius to realise their profession, which in jocular parlance was described as being 'on the game.' The landlord appeared to be on amiable terms with them, and it was obvious that their presence was on a regular footing.

Benjie approached them and obtained their business rates – which he relayed to me: remarkably reasonable, I thought, though I had neither intention nor inclination to avail myself of what was on offer.

After two drinks we decided to leave, Benjie having ascertained from one of the customers the name of a public house wherein a more lively atmosphere was promised, only five hundred yards distance from our present situation.

Named The Holly Bush it did indeed live up to our informant's boast. Rather select looking from the outside it did not prepare one for the debauched revelry going on inside. It was, in fact, what is nowadays known as a Gay Bar. This became immediately apparent to us on gaining entrance – though neither of us had even seen the like before. It was virgin territory to us, and as such possibly more astonishing because of that very fact.

It was jammed to capacity, the clientele mainly comprising incredibly exhibitionistic gays and lesbians, most of the gays sporting make-up and frilly blouses and bleached hair. Whilst the lesbians, apparently anxious to assert their masculinity, seemed to favour men's three-piece suits or jeans and shirts. Within this maelstrom of biologically maladjusted humanity we found ourselves gaping in disbelief. On stage a young man, in floral blouse and dangling earrings, was seated at a piano singing a version of 'Diamonds are a Girl's Best Friend' in a dedicated emulation of Marilyn Monroe, to be rapturously received by the audience, followed by a rather cumbersome lesbian who performed the old music-hall song 'I'm Burlington Bertie from Bow' to an almost equal reception.

Although neither Benjie or myself were attracted to the gay scene this occasion was, in its sheer novelty, a source of great fascination for us both.

Several other acts followed, all presented by a small fat man in a trilby hat, named 'Frankie.' Loose-lipped, tubby, and lecherous-looking, he was perhaps well-equipped to introduce the strange variety of humanity who had convinced themselves of their own talents. Leering and confidential in his approach he gave us no reason to doubt that his sexual voracity had encompassed every age, sex, and race to be found aboard this planet. Reticence was not his forté. As a stop-gap between the voluntary performers he entertained us with a string of jokes. The last were, in the main, so obscene, some also heavily racist, that even the 'broadest' of established comedians would have found them unacceptable.

An excitable and debauched-looking old man, with dyed black hair and a navy striped suit, button-holed Benjie and myself and, totally misreading us, explained that Saturday evening was the ultimate in value.

"Oo!" he murmured, in a curiously velvety voice, "Saturday night's the best here – some *lovely* boys get in here then – try and come."

"Fuck off!" replied Benjie, to his slight surprise, and we turned away.

It was by then eleven o'clock and we decided to leave – our minds in some turmoil at the course events had taken. It had not been our usual evening out!

The next morning I set out early, bagging-up with the energy and panache that only youth could provide. Without the company of Benjie and his non-stop judgements on the probable sexual prowess of the assorted stable-girls demanding my attention, I had completed the task in just over half an hour.

I followed my instinct upon approaching Brighton, turning off the main road into a tree-lined avenue to commence my calling. It was not easy, rebuffs coming thick and fast.

Indeed, one Jewish lady, still in hair-curlers, her features obscured by a substance resembling putty, and applied with little sense of economy; only her eyes were visible, gleaming malevolently at me from behind the front door – upon which I had knocked enthusiastically.

"So!" she exclaimed, "Where's the fire, already?"

Upon apprising her of the reason for my visit she turned on me in fury.

"Compost! Compost!" she shouted. "Why would I need compost from you? I've got two gardeners so why would I need you? I can live without your sort round here. Clear off!"

Her dismissal of me had about it a certain sign of character but lacked charm.

I eventually persuaded an ancient woman, tending her flower beds, that both she and her plants would benefit from a fulsome application. She purchased ten bags, thus starting me off on a mildly successful morning of small sales – one here, three there and half-a-dozen achieved twice. It was a morning in which the old adage 'Little Apples Taste Sweet' came into its own, and gradually my takings grew until, finally, I had managed to sell-out. (I might add here that I was on a lucky streak, lasting several weeks. Tiring but rewarding. Only once in all my years of 'calling' have I failed to dispose of even a single bag – a soul-destroying occurrence. Indeed, so disorientated was I by the experience that I convinced myself that I would never again make a sale! The next day, however, in a different town, I managed to disprove that pathetic conviction.)

By the time that all the bags had left the comfort of my lorry, I found it to be but twelve-thirty, so decided to seek out a small café which I had remembered for its eccentricity.

Named The Garden Café, it was not far from the town centre, on a side road. At that time it was run by a semi-hippy commune

166

consisting of two excitable young American boys, and a couple who were on the point of migrating to a smallholding situated in an almost unexplored region of Mid-Wales. It was their intention to become com-

pletely self-sufficient – inspired by the well-known practitioner of the life-style, John Seymour. They seemed a pleasant couple, he dread-locked and slight of figure, enshrouded in a mist of self-absorption, whilst his partner was the opposite: jovial, round of face and form and driven by optimistic ebullience. She was, one felt, the epitome of the legendary Earth Mother.

It was not long before I espied the café, its paintwork peeling, and with any vision of the interior interestingly obscured by the foliage of a multitude of large-leaved plants in terracotta pots, their growth uncurbed.

It was the kind of self-consciously 'rough and ready' eating establishment that would almost certainly be closed-down by over-zealous food inspectors today. Personally I felt that the ingestion of healthy food, even if produced in a free-spirited mode, was more beneficial than hygiene-driven victuals of a less nourishing kind, often from an over-varied menu.

The Garden's menu was vegetarian and limited to stews or cheese salads, with no more than one dessert – all offered at an extraordinarily low price. The clients were mostly of a faintly disturbed nature, though in no way actual lunatics.

Upon entering I was delighted to find that two of its most bizarre, though pleasant-natured patrons, were seated at separate tables.

The one of most eccentric aspect was known as Malc. Part of his unusual quality was emphasised by the fact of his having red hair worn in a single plait, two feet or more in length. This was echoed by his beard, also plaited to match. His dress habitually consisted of a top-hat, frock-coat, and blue jeans: it was the uniform he had adopted, which I found quite admirable. Diminutive of stature, almost pixie-like, his unvarying good humour assured him of acceptance. Residing in a one-up, one-down, terraced house, with the front door opening on to the pavement, he frequently offered passers-by cups of tea or even food, at no charge – merely goodwill – somewhat to their surprise.

The last I heard of him was that he had enticed an adventure-seeking hippy girl to accompany him on a trip to Lapland. They had, apparently, reached their destination, by sheer luck, their funds by then all but non-existent. Whereupon the young woman, to the chagrin of Malc, unceremoniously transferred her affections to one of the native Laplanders, whose attractions she found irresistible. And so it was that, after many complications, Malc found himself re-patriated back to Britain. He was, alas, one of those people from whom one derived most pleasure from just observing. His conversation was so fanciful and obscure that it was best allowed to fall upon deaf ears.

The other customer bore no resemblance to Malc. It was Hamilton Cobb, a remarkable figure of some six and a half feet tall and of no mean weight. It was rumoured that he was one of the few people for whom a course of steroids was prescribed at the age of fifteen in an effort to *restrain* his growth! He was a person of great peculiarity and, though only in his early thirties then, had about him an air of premature senility. Round of face, florid of complexion, he possessed thick brown hair which was a foot or more in length, swept back over his shoulders. Paradoxically he never appeared in public unless dressed in a clerical three-piece suit, collar and tie, and well-polished brogues. There was something faintly sinister one sensed about him. He was, one felt, a rare kind of asexual gay. A few years later I encountered him in the company of a German lady, of house-wifely appearance, who had, disastrously, persuaded him to subject himself to the hands of an over-enthusiastic barber. The latter's attentions were in no way improving. When I enquired as to the reason for this tonsorial folly, the German woman replied:

"Ach, Hamilton voss losing all his strength through ze hair, and he voss getting veaker and veaker."

"I see," I replied. "The opposite of Samson!"

Neither appeared to receive my acid comment very favourably. Hamilton, who had been reared by an elderly relative, was the recipient of a very small private income from shares bequeathed to him. He was thus happily removed from the life of S.S. benefits, or begging or stealing, which was the fate of many at that time who, for a variety of reasons, were unable to become absorbed into the world of regular work, at even the lowest level.

Hamilton resided in a spacious flat, on the second floor of a crumbling Victorian house in the area known as Kemp Town. Its decayed gentility and imposing size was echoed in every way by the gigantic frame of Hamilton himself. His suits, though all the work of bespoke tailoring, could scarcely boast that he was their first owner: even the best of his collection sat uneasily about his person, mostly with sleeves or trouser-legs either too short or too long, with true tastefulness managing to elude him.

Not content, alas, with the good fortune of being able to lead a life of complete leisure, even as a person of artificially advanced years, he was quite convinced of his talents as an artist, his works being executed in a curious combination of biro pen-work and vivacious colouration. His inability to recognize his limitations was in itself a minor tragedy.

With his flowing hair, remarkable stature, curiously out of date clothing, usually sporting a silver-topped walking stick, and, in inclement weather, a thick overcoat of subdued check worn cloak-like around his shoulders, he was a person not easily missed.

As a suspiciously asexual gay man it was difficult to fathom out the cause of his close union with the mouse-like German house-frau, on whose influence he seemed to rely even when it was patently misguided.

"But my dear boy," he beamed at me. "How lovely to see you – do sit with me and let me buy you a dish of herbal tea."

Malc smiled encouragingly at me from the next table, his lips, as ever, rather slow in their enunciation of the message he desired to impart. After expelling unrelated sentences, and sudden spurts of laughter, he eventually explained to me that he had spent the morning listening to the singing of Elizabeth Schwarzkopf on his wind-up gramophone!

"Cool, man, cool!" he gabbled, in a form of appreciation not commonly, one felt, applied to the work of the great singer.

Hamilton was in a magnanimous mood and insisted on treating me to a generously-filled bowl of lentil and vegetable stew, drawn by the well-endowed hippy girl from a large black cauldron simmering on a fiercely burning gas stove of obvious age. One imagined it as having served its apprenticeship in the back-kitchen of a lowly seaside boarding house, now nearing the end of its career.

The stew proved to be of very acceptable ingredients, the addition of numerous herbs adding considerably to its flavour.

Gradually other customers arrived, almost all of shabby and run-down aspect, both old and young, all examining the contents of their pockets or purses before placing an order – their enforced parsimony all too evident.

After a rather dilute conversation Hamilton left, telling me of his desire to complete his latest work in order to be able to despatch it to the Postmaster General, with the idea of it being accepted as a design for a postage stamp! Not an ambition, I felt sure, that would be fulfilled. But how would I know?

I was just absorbing the last drops of a cup of coffee when I was unexpectedly joined by a young woman of fairly attractive appearance, though her figure was loosely embraced by a duffle-coat of navy blue – scarcely the choice of a 'fashionista.'

We struck up a conversation, during which she enquired of my occupation, to my slight discomfort.

Thus at random, I replied: "I'm a house-breaker."

Unruffled by such a confession the young woman remained quite placid.

"What sort of houses do you break into?" she asked, without emotion.

"Well, whatever takes my fancy," I answered, noncommittally. "What do *you* do?" I enquired.

"I'm a stripper in a club," she replied calmly.

"Do you like doing it?" I said, innocently.

"It's good money – just for flashing me tits at dirty old men. I'm just going down the road to buy some new tassels – do you want to come with me?"

"Okay," I said, intrigued at the offer from a young woman of undoubted attraction, though carrying an over-worldly manner. It was my first experience of the 'Free Love' climate that was to develop with astonishing speed during the next decade or so. On our walk towards the 'Tassel Emporium' I deduced that the young woman, named Katie, was part of a somewhat dubious branch of the hippy movement which started out with such high ideals, before later, all too often, plunging from that path into drug-induced chaos.

Further discourse with the faintly unconscionable Katie hastened me to conclude that a sharp exodus on my part might be a wise move. I had no wish to become involved in what, at best, would have been a casual relationship. That was the indication I received from our conversation. The curiosity of our encounter was, for me anyway, its main interest value.

Outside the unimpressive entrance to the 'Tassel Emporium' I took my leave, promising to make contact through her 'phone number, with which I was supplied. In any event I felt un-impelled to avail myself of its service. The incident remained, affixed in my mind along with other trivia and flotsam – the jumbled memories of Life, one can only presume – both clogging and desultory.

After two or three weeks I could see that Benjie was pining for his extended family, anxious to heal the rift. With that in mind, he decided to make for Leicester, near which city he had learned that his father and mother, several brothers, and two sisters, were all stopping together on a piece of wasteland known as 'Gibberalta Rocks,' the last being misnamed after the nearest public house.

Although he suggested I move with him my mind was elsewhere, and also I felt no pull towards the County of Leicestershire – a place that held no good memories for me.

Thus Beshlie and I preferred to return to Southampton where, after a telephone call, it appeared within the bounds of possibility that we might engage in a transaction with the Bedford agent entailing the exchange of 'Pig's Head's' lorry for a brand new J-type vehicle, thereby achieving my main ambition of that moment.

And so it was, within a matter of a few hours, we were back on the dockside wasteland once more. I was pleased to see five or six trailers spread about the ground. I immediately recognized the turnout of Manuel Evans, 'Flash Herbert' and his son-in-law, 'Bib Bob,' with a brand new Eccles Traveller and new TK lorry, Olly and Polly, with a new J-type lorry and a neat little 'Carlight Special,' and two or three more lots with large *Gaujo* trailers and 3-ton Austin 'Lone Star' lorries. It was a good sight, and we pulled-in, with Manuel our closest neighbour.

Within twenty-four hours I had managed to clinch a deal – my new lorry would be ready for collection within a week. As an adventure in aesthetic presentation I ordered it to be finished in metallic bronze, with gold wings at front and rear. Whilst, in no way wishing to stint my desire for flamboyance, I ordered that the front radiator grille, bumper, and wing-mirrors should be chromed in the Travellers' fashion of the moment. As an added protection against anonymity I commissioned the body to be executed in the old-fashioned 'penny-farthing' wood – a legacy from the days of Romani waggons. With a handsome 'step' draw-bar it was a dream come true: such was the age of innocence.

In truth it was a wise and rewarding investment, its aspect appealing to all classes of Travellers – a passport into an ever-prospering world..... of which I was lucky enough to be able to take full advantage in the coming years....................

Author's Footnote

To those with an interest in the Travellers' 'Age of Mechanisation,' I can but direct them to my book BENEATH THE BLUE SKY published in 2007 and re-issued in 2012 by Five Leaves Publications. (Travellers' Life from 1960 to 2000)

Other Books by Dominic Reeve

Smoke in the Lanes 1958 and 2003

No Place Like Home 1961

Whichever Way we Turn 1965

Beneath the Blue Sky 2007 and 2012

Green Lanes and Kettle Cranes 2010

Lightning Source UK Ltd.
Milton Keynes UK
UKOW04f1933100917

308920UK00001B/51/P